THE
MYSTERY *of*
BAR KOKHBA

THE MYSTERY *of* BAR KOKHBA

An Historical and Theological Investigation of the Last King of the Jews

Leibel Reznick

JASON ARONSON INC.

Northvale, New Jersey

London

This book was set in 11 pt. Palacio by AeroType, Inc.

10 9 8 7 6 5 4 3 2 1

Library of Congress Cataloging-in-Publication Data

Reznick, Leibel.
    The mystery of Bar Kokhba : an historical and theological
investigation of the last king of the Jews / Leibel Reznick.
       p. cm.
    Includes bibliographical references and index.
    ISBN 1-56821-502-9 (alk. paper)
    1. Jews—History—Bar Kokhba Rebellion, 132–135. 2. Bar Kokhba,
d. 135. 3. Palestine—Antiquities. 4. Messiah—Judaism—History of
doctrines. I. Title.
DS122.8.R468 1996
937'.004924—dc20   95-45178

Manufactured in the United States of America. Jason Aronson Inc. offers books and cassettes. For information and catalog write to Jason Aronson Inc., 230 Livingston Street, Northvale, New Jersey 07647.

To
Rabbi David Reiss
to whom so many owe so much

Contents

Part III   The Jewish Doctrine of the Messiah

Acknowledgment

I would like to thank Rabbi Pinchus Rubinson for his many suggestions and comments striving to enhance the clarity of my manuscript. I would also like to thank my colleague, Rabbi N. Aryeh Feuer, for reviewing my notes and for his numerous recommendations. These two scholars are men of rare intellectual curiosity and insight. Once again I would like to pay tribute to Mr. Arthur Kurzweil and the staff of Jason Aronson Inc. for helping to bring this work to light.

I

BAR KOKHBA—
THE STORY

1

Introduction

The Holy Temple was destroyed. Jerusalem was in ruins. The First Revolt of the Jews against Rome had ended. The First Revolt began in 66 C.E. and was quashed by 73 C.E. with the capture of Masada. Every detail of this era was recorded by the contemporary Jewish historian Josephus Flavius. His chronicles of this horrific period aae still available to read and bemoan.

The next historical period in Judean history was the thirty-seven years from 99 C.E. to 135 C.E.. This is one of the most fascinating, enigmatic, and tragic epochs in Jewish history. It was the era of the Second and Third Revolts of the Jews, the massacre at Betar, and the mysterious Messiah—Bar Kokhba.

Alas, for this epoch of hope and horror there are no records. There was only one Roman historian who made any effort to capture this time period for posterity, Dio Cassius. Dio Cassius was born thirty years after the city of Betar had fallen so, unlike in the works of Josephus Flavius, we do not have a firsthand account of the events. Most of Dio Cassius's works have been lost and only a few extracts remain. Concerning the Bar Kokhba and Betar time period, there are a few brief paragraphs. There is no mention of Bar Kokhba by name, nor any mention of the city of Betar.

This era spanned the reigns of two Roman emperors, Trajan, 99 C.E.–117 C.E., and Hadrian, 117 C.E.–138 C.E.. Almost every detail of the chronology of those years in Jewish history has been debated in modern times by religious and secular historians. Although there are a score or so of references to particular incidents in the writings of our Sages, the name of the reigning emperor is often omitted. Even when the name is mentioned, the veracity of the name mentioned in the text is often called into question. Moreover, even when the text is deemed accurate, it is often impossible to fix an exact date to an event. Archaeological finds and historical evidence have shed little light in this area. The catastrophic climax of the Bar Kokhba era occurred in the ancient city of Betar, which has yet to be excavated and examined by the archaeological community.

With these facts in mind, in the next six chapters I shall try, as well as possible, to reconstruct the history of this era. I shall try to avoid any controversy of substantive issue in order to familiarize the reader with our subject, the messianic hero— Bar Kokhba. Once the reader is then familiar with the topic, in subsequent chapters we shall examine more closely the records of the rabbinical texts and scrutinize the few archaeological discoveries that have been uncovered with regards to this matter to see what phenomenal revelations they hold in store for us.

2

Star of Jacob

Nothing is known of the family and early life of the charismatic Shimon bar Kosiba. Even his exact name was not known until recent times. The great Sage and spiritual leader of the Jewish people, Rebbe Akiva, upon witnessing the almost supernatural military skills of Shimon bar Kosiba, proclaimed Shimon to be the divinely appointed savior of the Jews. Shimon bar Kosiba was the Messiah.[1]

Rebbe Akiva had taught that, based on the prophecy of Haggai—"It shall be one small while, and I will shake heaven and earth,"[2] the "Golus without end" would be short-lived. A king from Judah would arise and he would deliver the Jews. Rebbe Akiva believed Bar Kosiba to be that King of Judea.[3]

Rebbe Akiva called Bar Kosiba "Bar Kokhba," "the son of the star," referring to the biblical verse, "A star has arisen in Jacob."[4] The majority of the Sages agreed with Rebbe Akiva and recognized Bar Kokhba as the Messiah.[5] A few, more skeptical, Sages called him "Bar Koziba," "the son of deceit," for they distrusted Bar Kokhba's integrity. Rebbe Yochanan ben Torta rejoined, "Akiva, grass will sooner grow on your chin, before the Messiah comes."[6]

Jews flocked from all corners of the Roman empire to stand under the banner of Bar Kokhba. Indeed, 400,000 inspired Jews answered the call.[7] They left their homes and possessions to learn the ways of war, and 200,000 were put to the test of courage of biting off the end of their finger.[8] The Sages objected to the self-mutilation and suggested a test of uprooting a sapling while riding at full gallop. Another 200,000 passed this test.[9]

In the days of old, the prophet Jeremiah had warned the Jewish people against four things: do not rebel against the government, do not try to hasten the End of Days, do not reveal the mysteries of Torah, and do not leave the Diaspora by force; otherwise, why should the Messiah have to come? Bar Kokhba did not heed the warning and tried to hasten the end of days by force, proclaiming himself to be the Messiah.[10]

3

Trajan and the Second Revolt (99 C.E.–117 C.E.)

I t is not known for certain when the rise of Bar Kokhba began. One thing is certain; the messianic aspirations of the Jewish masses had their roots in the Second Revolt of the Jews against Rome. This occurred during the reign of the emperor Trajan, about forty-five years after the First Revolt. The First Revolt (68 C.E.–73 C.E.) had culminated in the destruction of the Second Temple and the devastation of Jerusalem; but the resilient spirit of the Jewish People was still very much alive.

The sixty-year-old Trajan envisioned himself to be the Alexander of Rome. He first subdued the European provinces surrounding the Danube. He then sought to annex the land between the Euphrates and the Ganges rivers, as Alexander had done before him. The only resistance Trajan encountered was from the Jews who lived in these Asiatic provinces.

The Jews occupied whole towns in the lands sustained by the Tigris and Euphrates rivers and had enjoyed a certain amount of autonomy. They had their own religious and political leaders, who stood steadfast, blocking the path of the conquering Trajan. The town of Netzivon, whose religious leader was the renowned Sage, Rebbe Yehuda ben Bisayra, offered such resistance that a long siege was required before the inhabitants finally yielded. The district of Adiabene, on the Tigris, whose rulers had converted to Judaism one hundred years earlier, put up a galant struggle. But they, too, succumbed to the superior Roman forces. By the winter of 115 c.e., much of Mesopotamia and her Jews had yielded to the Romans.

Trajan was not content with simply having the Jews under his dominion. He wanted them to socially and religiously assimilate into the ranks of the pagan Romans. Trajan's victory was designed, not merely to be a conquest of lands, but rather to embody the triumph of Roman culture.

Springtime brings with it a renewed spirit of life. The earth blossoms forth, resurrected from the dead of winter. By the spring of 116 c.e., the Jews had revived their zealous determination and once again rose up in rebellion to defend their beliefs and heritage.

The Jews of Mesopotamia, present-day Iraq, and Judea were the first to revolt. The Judeans, under the leadership of the two righteous brothers, Lulianus and Pappus, drove out the Roman officials. The military garrisons were destroyed. News of the rebellion and it successes gave courage to the Jews of northern Africa. Jews in Egypt, Libya, and Cyprus revolted and cast off the bonds of Rome.

The African revolt began in Cyrenaica, Libya. Exaggerated Gentile reports claimed that the Jews had massacred 220,000 Romans. (The devastation was so great that in later years new colonists had to be brought in to populate the area.) From Libya, the revolt spread to Egypt. In the Egyptian capital, Alexandria, the fighting was especially fierce. Anti-Jewish riots broke out and many Jews were tortured and massacred. The Alexandrian Jews, with the help of their Libyan brothers, avenged the blood of the slain, and the remnant Romans and Greeks fled by boat up the Nile.

From Egypt, the revolt spread to Cyprus in the Mediterranean Sea. Cyprus had a large Jewish population, and, led by a man called Artemion, the Jews defeated their pagan oppressors. Exaggerated reports placed the Roman casualties at a quarter million. The Cyprian capital was totally destroyed.

The Jews, jubilant with their victories, had visions of rebuilding Judea and the Holy Temple. The "exile without end" would have lasted only forty-five years. The intrepid spirit that accompanies triumph gave rise to the hope of the messianic dream.

Understandably, Trajan did not share in the hopes and aspirations of the Jews. Trajan dedicated his egomaniacal ambition into turning the vision and dream of the Jews into a nightmare. He placed two of his most trusted and bloodthirsty generals, Martius Turbo and Lucius Quietus, in charge of subduing the Jewish revolt. Turbo was placed in charge of the African campaign and Quietus took charge of the Judean and Mesopotamian fronts. Quietus was given orders to entirely annihilate the Jewish population. The sadistic Quietus welcomed the opportunity with glee.

The flames of Jewish passion were fueled by their dreams; but dreams are not always a match for military prowess. Slowly and methodically, Turbo put down the African revolt. In Egypt, tens of thousands of Jews were slaughtered and butchered. The Great Synagogue of Alexandria, one of the great architectural wonders of the ancient world, was destroyed. In Cyprus, no Jew remained on the island alive. As one historian wrote, "Their blood dyed the sea red."[1] A law was decreed that no Jew might ever set foot again on the island.

The barbaric Quietus likewise was successful in ending the rebellion in Judea and Mesopotamia. He conducted a war of annihilation against the Jews. The bodies of the slain Jewish men blocked the streets and byways of the Middle Eastern cities and towns. The Jewish women were assured that they would be spared if only they would give themselves to the Roman soldiers. However, the Jewish wives and daughters said, "Do to us as you have done to our husbands and fathers." And so, the blood of the women mingled with the blood of the men.[2]

The Jewish vision of a divinely inspired messianic king ruling all mankind from the Temple of Peace in Jerusalem was dashed. When the clouds of battle dispersed, the "son of David" had not set his throne in the City of God; rather, it was the wicked Quietus, because of his unholy success, who was rewarded with the governorship of Judea. He was granted unlimited powers. It was Quietus who ruled over the still-desolate Temple Mount. The Second Revolt had ended.

This was not a time for the realization of dreams. Trajan's aspiration of a conquest to the Ganges was never realized. As the emperor lay on his deathbed, he expressed his final wish that Quietus be given the title of emperor. However, Trajan's wife, Plotina, informed Rome that Trajan wished his nephew, Aelius Hadrian, to be his heir and successor.

4

Hadrian and the Third Revolt (117 C.E.–135 C.E.)

Hadrian, like his uncle Trajan, was born in Spain (see Plate 1). Hadrian had commanded Trajan's troops in Syria during the Mesopotamian campaign. He had witnessed how his uncle tried to extinguish the spirit of the Jews by slaughter and persecution. Now that the reins of power had been turned over to him, Hadrian was unsure how the Jews would react. He feared they would renew their determination to rebel and shake off the yoke of Rome. Hadrian decided that a different tactic was needed. It was this tactic that once again encouraged the seeds of the unfulfilled messianic fervor to germinate and blossom forth.

Hadrian removed the evil Quietus from the governorship of Judea. Upon Quietus's return to Rome, Hadrian had him executed. Hadrian then sought to rebuild the Holy City anew. The new Judean capital would be a gift of appeasement from Rome to her Jews. Throughout the empire, the Jews were to be considered and treated as any other citizen. Lulianus and Pappus, the two brothers who had instigated the revolt against Trajan, were appointed as public officials to oversee the needs of the Jews. Onkylos, the convert,

Plate 1 Hadrian.

was placed in charge of the rebuilding of Jerusalem. Funds were raised throughout the Middle East to help ease the burdens created by the previous years of persecution and devastation.

Under Trajan, the messianic hope had stirred in spite of the Roman emperor. Now, under Hadrian, the messianic longing was encouraged by the emperor himself. The Jews interpreted the overtures of peace as a heavenly sign that the Messianic Era was approaching. Almost confirming their belief, a decree came from Rome granting the Jews permission to rebuild their Temple. The Jews celebrated.

Even Hadrian celebrated the newfound mutual respect between Judea and Rome. He had coins minted showing the Roman emperor and the "widow Jerusalem" standing near an altar on which both were preparing to offer a sacrifice.

The presence of the Roman soldiers in Judea was only to maintain the peace. The Jewish blacksmiths and metalworkers were given the task of making the weapons for these foreign legionnaires. The suspicious, if not prophetic, Jews feared that one day these weapons would be turned against them and purposely made them weak. The weapons would make a grand display but would be almost useless in battle.

The favor bestowed upon the Jews stirred the jealousy and anger of the Christians living in the Holy Land. They feared that if the Temple were to be rebuilt and the Sanhedrin (religious supreme court) be given authority over the land, they would be threatened. A Christian delegation informed Rome that building a Temple in Jerusalem would only encourage the Jews to rebel.[1]

Hadrian feared to rescind the permission to build the Temple; therefore, he decreed that it be built elsewhere, or at least that its original dimensions be altered. The Jews, realizing that the Temple could not be built anywhere other than on Mount Moriah and following the dimensions as instructed by the prophets of old, understood that Hadrian had withdrawn permission for the Temple to be built.[2]

Many Jews from the Diaspora had already gathered in the land of their forefathers and dedicated their efforts to prepare for the Temple reconstruction. When the news reached them that they were to cease all labors with regard to this matter, they were determined to revolt. The Sages, fearing the outcome of a doomed revolt, sent Rebbe Yehoshua ben Chananiah to calm the people.[3]

The daughter of Hadrian was found murdered and the Jews were accused of the crime. The ire of Hadrian raged at the Jews. If the culprits were not found, all the Jews would suffer. Lulianus and Pappus "confessed" to the ill deed in order to save their brethren. Hadrian had these two righteous brothers executed in the city of Lud.[4]

5

The Great Persecution

The conciliatory policies of Hadrian toward the Jews came to an abrupt halt. Several factors contributed to the sudden change in attitude. Hadrian's desire for revenge for the murder of his daughter was in no way satisfied by the execution of the two brothers, who had righteously confessed out of the noble desire to protect their countrymen. Civil unrest was also stirring among the rival sects in Judea. The Christians and Samarians were agitated by the perceived favoritism shown to the Jews.

Perhaps the strongest element that brought about the change was that the natives of the other conquered provinces adopted the Roman lifestyle and culture as their own. However, the faithful Jews tenaciously held onto their traditional ways and beliefs. Hadrian, like his uncle Trajan, was now prepared to wage a religious and cultural war against the Jews. The Sages viewed this confrontation as a renewed fight between Jacob and the angel of Essau. The Children of Jacob and Hadrian, the descendant of Essau, would once again do battle for the supremacy of the human spirit.[1]

Hadrian issued many anti-Semitic decrees. In order to limit the Jewish population of Judea, it was forbidden for any foreign Jew to emigrate to the Holy Land. In order to put an end to the religious and cultural identity of the Jews, it was decreed that the Jews were forbidden to observe the rites of circumcision and the laws of the Sabbath and family purity.[2] A violation of any decree was punishable by death. Any Gentile seeking conversion was also subject to the same penalty.

To add insult to injury, it was decreed that no Jew was permitted to enter Jerusalem and that the head of a swine was to be placed over the southern gate of the city.

Hadrian issued one more decree that pushed the Jews beyond the point of tolerance. He ordered that a pagan temple be built on the Temple Mount. The conditions for a Judean uprising and the seeds of the Third Revolt were now present. All that was lacking was a military leader to lead the revolt. Such a savior then came upon the scene.

6

Bar Kokhba

It was at this time that Bar Kokhba seems to have appeared out of the mist of time. His miraculous victories, vanquishing the Romans, driving them out of Jerusalem, and chasing them to the far corners of Judea, made him the hero that the Jewish people so desperately needed. The approbation from Rebbe Akiva and the Sages gave the Jews the Messiah for whom they had so longed.

The fleeing Roman governor of Judea, Tinnius Rufus (called by the Jews, Tyrannus Rufus—Rufus the Terrible), was powerless against the forces of Bar Kokhba. The Roman emperor, Hadrian, sent two generals to come to the aid of Tinnius Rufus, Publius Marcellus and Lolius Urbicius. They brought legions from Phoenicia, Arabia, and Egypt. But even these ablest of military men could not subdue the messianic fervor. Within a year's time, Bar Kokhba had recaptured 985 villages and constructed 50 fortresses. Bar Kokhba and his army of 580,000 dedicated warriors seemed invincible.

Confident of total victory, Bar Kokhba had Roman coins restruck. The new coins proclaimed, "Freedom of Jerusalem" and "Freedom of Israel."

Hadrian, who had expected a quick end to the revolt, was becoming the object of mockery. In Britain, too, he was faced with a revolt, but Julius Severus ended Britannia's hopes of freedom. Hadrian called Severus to the Judean front and ordered that Judea be recaptured and subdued.

Upon Severus's arrival in Judea, he saw that there was no single battlefront. The entire land had to be recaptured. He therefore resolved himself not to expect a quick victory. His troops went from city to city and from town to town, besieging the inhabitants and murdering the captives.

Julius Severus had promised amnesty to all those Jews who surrendered. Many Jews, seeing the successes of the Romans, feared that the Messiah had indeed not yet arrived, and so they surrendered. Many Jews were taken to the Valley of Rimmon. Severus ordered, "Before I finish my cake and leg of fowl, see to it that not one Jew remains alive." The soldiers complied, and a terrible massacre took place in the valley.[1]

The tide was turning against Bar Kokhba. He blamed God for his losses and declared, "God, if You do not march with us, then also do not march against us."[2] The great Sages, who had endorsed Bar Kokhba as the illustrious savior, began to have their doubts.

During the campaigns of Julius Severus, Rebbe Akiva was captured, imprisoned, and suffered a martyr's death.

It took Severus several years and more than fifty battles to recapture Judea. When Jerusalem was retaken by the Romans, the governor, Tinnius Rufus, brought a plow to the Temple Mount and plowed it up. That occurred on the ninth day of Av.[3] In the end, all Judean cities and strongholds were recaptured except one, Betar. Betar became the one last haven for the Jews, and it was in Betar that Bar Kokhba, the Star of Jacob, would fall.[4]

7

Son of Deceit

The great city of Betar was the last refuge of the Jews (see Plate 2). It was southwest of Jerusalem, not far from the Mediterranean Sea. It was surrounded on three sides by steep valleys, which provided a natural barrier against invasion. It had its own wellspring within the city. An invader would be unable to cut off the water supply. Moreover, a strong wall surrounded the city, making it almost invincible.

Betar had been a center for Torah studies, with hundreds of Houses of Learning, each with hundreds of students. Betar was a city that was at peace with itself.

The people of Betar were confident that Bar Kokhba would miraculously deliver them from the Roman threat. Schoolchildren would mock the Romans, saying, "Should they come against us, we will stab them with our pens."[1]

During the three-year siege of Betar, Rebbe Elazer of Modim, the uncle of Bar Kokhba, fasted and prayed, "Lord of the Universe, sit not in judgment today." The emperor, Hadrian, was weary of waiting for the city to surrender and prepared to withdraw the troops. Rebbe Elazer's prayers had almost

Plate 2 The ruins of Betar. *Copyright ©1991 Richard Nowitz.*

been answered when a traitorous old Jew told Hadrian: "As long as that pious rooster crows you will not be able to overtake the city. But wait, do not withdraw, I shall enable you to conquer the city this very day."[2]

The traitor entered the city and found Rebbe Elazer engaged in prayer. He pretended to whisper something into the Sage's ear. The people saw the traitor conversing with Rebbe Elazer and reported it to Bar Kokhba. Bar Kokhba had the traitor brought before him and demanded to know what had transpired between him and Rebbe Elazer. The traitor said: "If I tell you, the Emperor Hadrian will kill me. If I do not tell, you will kill me. Better I die at your hand. Rebbe Elazer said that he wants to surrender Betar to the Romans."[3]

Bar Kokhba had his uncle, Rebbe Elazer, brought before him. The uncle claimed he knew of no conversation with that man, for he had been engrossed in his prayers. Bar Kokhba flew into a rage, kicked the holy Sage, and killed him. The very life and breath of Betar was extinguished.[4]

The Sages had an oral tradition that the Messiah could smell truth. They decided to test this Messiah. A case was brought before Bar Kokhba, and he sat in judgment. The Messiah ruled incorrectly; he could not smell truth. And so, the Sages killed the Messiah.[5] Betar was conquered, and the head of Bar Kokhba was brought to Hadrian.[6]

With the death of Bar Kokhba, the walls of Betar were no longer impenetrable. The city fell, and the slaughter that followed was unimaginable. Men, women, and children were murdered with equal abandon. The tragedy of Betar equaled the destruction of the Temple.[7] Besides those who succumbed to hunger, a half million Jews were slaughtered. Like the destruction of the First and Second Temples, the destruction of Betar also occurred on the ninth day in the month of Av.[8]

The tens of thousands of schoolchildren, who had threatened to stave off the Romans with their pens, were wrapped in their scrolls and burned alive. Only a single child managed to escape—Shimon ben Gamliel.[9]

Roman battalions were set up along the main roads of Judea to capture and execute the fleeing survivors of the holocaust. Many Jews stayed off the roads and sought refuge in the mountain caves. These refugees had little or no food, and starvation began to take its course. In desperation, they fed on the corpses of their fallen brothers.[10]

Captives were dragged off by the thousands and sold in the slave markets of Gaza and Hebron. There were so many offered for sale that the price of a Judean slave fell to a few meager coins. Many were taken on ships to Egypt to be sold. Not all these captives made it to the land where their forefathers were enslaved. Many ships sunk because they were overburdened with their human cargo. Many other Jews succumbed to hunger and starvation.

Jerusalem was rebuilt as a Roman garrison. The name of the once proud and noble city was changed to Aelia Capitolina so that Jerusalem the Holy would be forgotten. Inside the northern gate, a great column was erected with a larger-than-life statue of the emperor Hadrian standing on it in a pose of victory. Upon the Temple Mount, a pagan temple was erected to the god Jupiter
soldiers stood on the steps of their pagan temple and celebrated the end of the conquest of Judea.

II

BAR KOKHBA IN HISTORY AND ARCHAEOLOGY

8

Dio Cassius

There is nothing like firsthand reportage to students of history. Though it may lack the unbiased sobriety of hindsight, instead it contains and conveys the intensity of emotion prevalent at the time. The era of Bar Kokhba was certainly filled with high-pitched emotions on both sides. The Jewish Nation was stirred with the hopes brought by the messianic fervor. The Roman Empire had its enviable cultural reputation to defend. But alas, there are no existent firsthand reports to convey the complex sentiments of that era.

One of the primary secular sources of information concerning the Bar Kokhba Era comes from the writings of Dio Cassius. Born in 163 C.E., this chronicler of ancient Rome wrote eighty books, most of which have been lost. He began his monumental project in 239 C.E., over one hundred years after Betar had fallen. The little material that remains today is in extracts quoted by medieval scholars.

Concerning the Third Revolt in Judea, Dio Cassius writes:

Hadrian founded in Jerusalem a city in place of the one that had been razed to the ground, naming it Aelia Capitolina. On the

site of the Jewish Temple he raised a new temple to Jupiter. This
brought on a war of no slight importance nor of brief duration.
For the Jews deemed it intolerable that foreign races should
settle in their city and foreign religious rites be planted there.[1]

In this paragraph, Dio Cassius is attributing the Third Revolt
of the Jews against Rome, which occurred under Hadrian, to
the founding of Aelia Capitolina and the building of the Temple to Jupiter. It was that intolerable offense that spurred the
Jews to revolt. Accordingly, the founding of Aelia Capitolina
would have been circa 122 c.e.

However, Eusebius of Caesarea, a third-century church historian, writes, "In the twentieth year of Hadrian [136 c.e.]
Aelia was founded. In front of the gate, by the road which
leads to Bethlehem, he set up an idol of a pig in marble,
signifying the subjugation of the Jews to Roman authority."[2]
Eusebius is stating that Aelia Capitolina was not established
until after the Third Revolt was quashed in 132–133 c.e. It was
not the cause for the revolt; rather, it was the terrible result of
the failed insurrection.

The Talmud states that the Roman government decreed that
the Jews were forbidden to observe the Sabbath, the rites of
circumcision, and the laws of family purity.[3] Doros HaRishonim writes that these laws were passed by Hadrian.[4] He
further asserts that it was these anti-Semitic decrees that
prompted the Jews to revolt against Rome; moreover, it was
not until after the revolt had been put down that the pagan
temple was built on the Temple Mount.

Perhaps the contradiction between Dio Cassius and Eusebius can be resolved by explaining (as stated in the previous
chapters) that Hadrian first suggested the plan to build a
pagan temple in 122 c.e. The very thought of such an unholy
violation of the Temple Mount pushed the Jews to rebel. After
the rebellion was put down, in 132–133 c.e., the pagan temple
was actually built.

Dio Cassius continues: "So long as Hadrian was close by in Egypt and Syria, the Jews remained quiet. The [Jewish smiths] were called upon to furnish the Roman soldiers with weapons. They purposely made them of poor quality so the [weapons] would be rejected and they may have use of them themselves."[5] Dio Cassius claims that the Jews made weapons of poor quality so the Romans would reject them and the Jews would have use of them. This seems somewhat illogical. Why would the Jews want poorly constructed weapons? The more rational explanation is that the Jews suspected that the weapons would one day be used against them. Therefore, they did not wish to give the enemy ammunition.

Dio Cassius continues:

> When [Hadrian] went farther away, they openly revolted. To be sure, the Jews did not dare to confront the Romans in the open field, but rather they occupied the advantageous positions in the country. They fortified their positions with walls and tunnels in order to have refuge whenever needed. The Jews would meet unobserved under ground. They pierced these subterranean passages from above at intervals to let in air and light.[6]

The subterranean tunnels and passages referred to here will be the fascinating subject of our next chapter.

Dio Cassius continues: "All Judea had been stirred up. Many other nations joined them for personal gain. The whole earth, one might say, was stirred up in the matter."[7] From here we see that the Bar Kokhba revolt was not some insignificant local rebellion but rather had a worldwide effect, both politically and militarily. Later, Dio Cassius says that when Hadrian wrote to the Senate, he omitted the standard greeting, "If you and your children are in health, it is well. I and the legions are in health," because of the massive losses suffered by the Roman troops. Though the battlefront was centered in Judea, the effect of the Bar Kokhba rebellion was felt throughout the

Roman Empire. This only adds to the mystery of why so little historical evidence remains of this epoch.

> Hadrian set forth his best generals. First was Julius Severus who was dispatched from Britain, where he was governor. Severus did not attack his opponents out in the open, in view of their great numbers and determination, but intercepted small groups. He surrounded them and deprived them of food, exposing his troops to little danger. Very few of them survived.
>
> Fifty of their most important outposts and 985 of their famous villages were razed to the ground. Slain in battle and various raids were 580,000. It is impossible to determine those who perished by famine, disease, and fire. Thus nearly all of Judea was made desolate.
>
> The monument of Solomon, which the Jews venerate, fell to pieces and collapsed. Wolves and hyenas rushed howling into the cities.

It is not clear what Dio Cassius calls the "monument of Solomon." It is usually understood by scholars to mean King Solomon's tomb. Another possibility is that it is an appelation for the Temple of the Jews. However, the Temple had already been destroyed by Vespasian and Titus in 70 c.e. Later in our investigation into the Bar Kokhba story, we shall investigate the compelling evidence suggesting that Bar Kokhba rebuilt the fallen Temple.

9

The Underground War

I n the preceding chapter, Dio Cassius mentioned the underground installations of the Bar Kokhba revolutionaries. Though these tunnels merited only a few brief passages in Dio Cassius's work, they gave evidence of the resourcefulness and dedication of the Jews, and they shall be the subject of this chapter.

The first underground installation was accidently discovered in 1978, by an inspector for the Israel Department of Antiquities who was looking into reports of tomb robbing by Arab villagers. By 1988, over 300 of these subterranean complexes had been found in the foothills of the Judean Desert, mainly to the southwest of Jerusalem.

The Jewish revolutionaries created two types of underground structures beneath the desert sands. One type was built to accommodate a large family and would be used as a temporary shelter in case of an enemy presence. The second, more impressive, type was like an underground village. These were equipped with large cisterns to hold precious water, great storage rooms, and meeting rooms with stone benches. The many chambers were joined by low, interconnecting tunnels, so low that, in some instances, one had to crawl on all fours to pass

Plate 3 Olive press in an underground installation. *Copyright ©1991 Richard Nowitz.*

through them. The installations were usually located beneath the buildings of a settlement. The secret entrances could be blocked from the inside to prevent enemy penetration.

These hideouts also served as fortresses and were often built on a hill or high ridge. From these outposts, the revolutionaries would attack Roman forces who were traveling from city to city. By limiting travel, the revolutionaries blocked the delivery of vital supplies to the Romans who occupied the cities.

The entrances to these chalky brown bunkers were quite small, about two feet square. The entrance would be from inside a cave or under the floors of public buildings or private homes. Some were hidden behind olive presses and, in one instance, an entrance was found in a pigeon coop (see Plate 3).

Inside the complex, there were also means to block off one section from another in case an invader managed to pierce the

Plate 4 Passageway in an underground installation. *Copyright ©1991 Richard Nowitz.*

main entrance. The various chambers of a single installation were located on different levels. The inhabitants would have to climb single-file up or down a narrow shaft to get to the next level. An enemy climbing through a shaft would need both hands to climb. He would not be able to use a weapon and would, therefore, be most vulnerable.

In some cases, the upper level could only be reached by climbing a rope ladder, which led to an opening in a high ceiling. When the last person had climbed through the opening, the ladder was withdrawn and the hole was sealed with a large stone held in place by wooden beams from behind.

An occasional shaft in the roof of a chamber would allow fresh air and some light to enter. Oil lamps were used to supply additional lighting (see Plate 4).

How much success these determined Jews had is not known. Some historians believe that the underground structures were built during the early stages of the Bar Kokhba uprising. If so, they certainly had a degree of success as Bar Kokhba did eventually drive out the Romans from the cities of Judea. Other historians believe that the installations were constructed during the waning years of the revolt. They see these tunnels as an act of desperation by soon-to-be defeated warriors. However, it is the view of this author that they were built during the early years of the revolt.

We do know that in the end, the Bar Kokhba revolutionaries were defeated. But these installations give evidence to the ingenuity and perseverance of a people inspired by the messianic hope.

10

Herodium

Dio Cassius mentioned that Bar Kokhba had fifty outposts under his command. The term *outpost*, as used in American frontier vernacular, conjures up the image of a rather small, almost forsaken, building surrounded by a stockade fence. Lest you think these outposts were also of insignificant nature and makeshift structure, I shall describe what is known of one of these outposts, Herodium, which, according to some historians, was the capital of Bar Kokhba's desert empire (see Plate 5). It will attest to the regal splendor befitting the messianic king.

Herodium, which is located seven miles south of Jerusalem, was constructed by the Judean king Herod around 23 B.C.E. During his lifetime, it served as Herod's royal palace and fortress. After his death, Herod was buried in Herodium. His tomb has still not been found.

Herodium is an artificial mountain 330 feet high. From afar it bears a striking resemblance to a volcano. The "crater" of Herodium is 200 feet across. Surrounding the rim of the crater are two concentric walls. They were 90 feet high and 11½ feet apart. Between the walls were five stories of rooms and halls.

Plate 5 Herodium. *Copyright ©1989 Richard Nowitz.*

Built into the walls were four great towers, facing the four directions of the compass. Three of the towers were shaped like half-silos, with their curved sides facing outward, while the east tower was completely round. The upper portions of these 130-foot-high towers contained five floors with four rooms on each floor.

Inside the artificial crater was an opulent complex, the eastern half of which was completely occupied by a royal garden surrounded by marble columns. The splendor of the verdant foliage contrasted with the desert sands below.

The western half of the crater contained three buildings. The southern building was a 50-foot-long hall, probably a dining hall, with beautiful mosaic flooring. The Bar Kokhba rebels later converted this hall into a synagogue. The center building, the largest of the three, contained many rooms, which presumably served as the main living and sleeping quarters. The northern building was a five-room, luxurious bathhouse, which contained an entrance room and separate dressing area. There was a steam room (caldarium) with a barrel-vaulted ceiling. The hot bath (tepidarium) was a circular room with a domed ceiling. The cold bath (frigidarium) and all the other rooms had colorful frescoes painted on the walls and beautiful mosaic floors.

Access to the crater from the desert floor was by way of a 500-foot-long stairway, which was 20 feet wide. The first 300 feet went up the slope of the "volcano." The stairway then pierced through the mountain, and the remaining 200 feet of the stairway ascended through the mountain itself.

There were four large water cisterns located deep inside the mountain. Their total capacity was over 750,000 gallons.

Bar Kokhba's rebels built an intricate underground complex deep inside the crater. So far, over 1,000 feet of tunnels and chambers have been discovered. The tunnels that connect the underground rooms are 4½ feet wide and 6 feet high. In some places, the ceilings of the subterranean chambers are as high as 43 feet.

Near the base of the mountain was a huge building of unknown purpose. It was 425 feet long and 180 feet wide, with barrel-vaulted ceilings. In front of this building was a 1,100-foot-long terrace.

A short way across the desert from this building was a remarkable complex, the centerpiece of which was an artificial lake, 230 feet long and 150 feet wide, with an island in the center. The pool was fed by an aqueduct 3½ miles long, which brought water from a spring outside Bethlehem. A marble-columned pavilion stood on the island. The pool was surrounded by royal gardens which, in turn, were surrounded by marble columns supporting a roof. Outside the columns was an ornately decorated wall. The eastern and western sides of the gardens were flanked by two halls, each 360 feet long.

To the northeast of the pool and gardens was another complex of buildings encompassing a greater area than the pool and gardens themselves. To the southeast was a large structure spanning 2,400 square feet. To the southwest was a lavish, nine-room bathhouse. Nearby was a large mikva.

This was the regal splendor and strength that served as Bar Kokhba's main outpost, which befitted the messianic king. Moreover, Herodium was only one of fifty such outposts.

11

Bar Kokhba Letters

Spoken words carry with them a bit of the speaker's soul. The words that are chosen are like bricks and the phrases that are constructed reveal the architecture of the intellect and the design of the psyche. It is vital when studying an individual to examine his words as well as his deeds. Until now we have been focusing on the actions and events of the Bar Kokhba Era. If only we could examine the utterances of the charismatic Messiah. Amazingly enough, we can.

Several written communications bearing the name of Shimon Bar Kokhba have been found in the caves of the Judean Desert in the south of Israel.

indicating different scribes. Whether any one of them was actually written by Bar Kokhba himself cannot be determined. However, it is evident that, at the very least, Bar Kokhba dictated the letters. All the letters are very brief, to the point, and businesslike. There is no flowery language or superfluous words. They reveal no signs of hope or despair. He uses no title to indicate his superior station. There is no harshness of tone nor tone of compassion. What this tells us about the hero of the revolution, I leave to the armchair psychologists. But these letters, more than anything else, bring back to life the messianic hero of the failed revolution.

Perhaps the most fascinating letter was written shortly before the festival of Succos and shows the religious zeal and dedication that Shimon displayed. The festival ritual required the "four species," namely the citron, palm branch, myrtle, and willow. The last three mentioned were bound together and held with the citron while blessings and the praises in the book of Psalms were recited (see Plate 6).

Bar Kokhba was in dire need of these four species, and the holiday was fast approaching when he wrote this letter, which is written in Aramaic (based on a translation by Y. Yadin):

> Shimon.
> To Yehuda bar Menashe
> To Kiryat Arabaya
>
> I have sent two donkeys. You shall send two men with them to Yehonathan bar Be'ayan and to Masabla. They shall pack and bring back to you palm branches and citrons.
> You should send others from your place to bring back myrtles and willows. See that they are tithed. Send them [all] to [my] camp. [Our] army is large. Peace.[1]

We do not know who Yehuda bar Menashe was, nor do we know where Kiryat Arabaya was located.

Yehonathan and Masabla are well known from other period letters. They were lieutenants of rebels forces in Ein Gedi. Why this letter and the two donkeys were not sent directly to Ein Gedi is not known. The fact that Bar Kokhba had to send donkeys shows that beasts of burden were not a common commodity among the rebel forces.

The letter instructs Yehuda to tithe the citrons. Obviously, Bar Kokhba was not relying on Yehonathan and Masabla to do

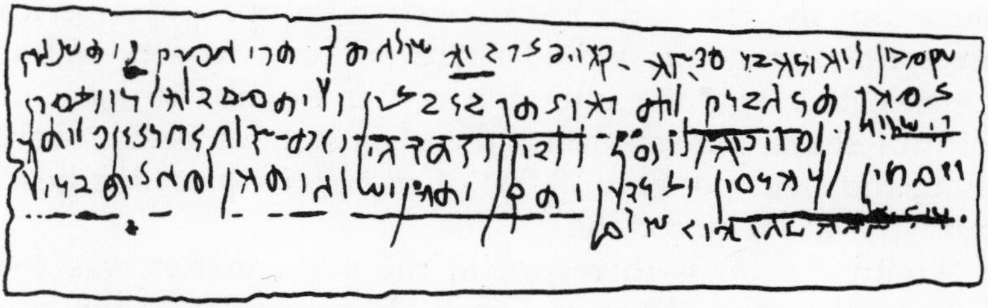

Plate 6 The "Four Species Letter."

the task. In talmudic literature, produce that leaves the hands of an ignoramus is termed "demai." It is questionable if the ignoramus separated the required tithes. The Talmud raises the question of whether demai citrons can be used in the festival rite.[2] The House of Shammai ruled that they are unfit for the ritual. The House of Hillel ruled that they may be used. The law is in accordance with the House of Hillel that the demai citrons may be used for the ritual.

If the demai citrons could be used, according to the ruling of the House of Hillel, why did Bar Kokhba insist that Yehuda himself separate the tithes? There is a tradition, often quoted in the name of Rabbi Yitzchok Ashkenasi, the sainted seventeenth-century kabbalist known as the Ari, that in the time of the Messiah, the rulings will no longer follow the House of Hillel, but rather, the law will be in accordance with the opinion of the House of Shammai. Since Bar Kokhba believed that he was the true messiah, we can readily understand that he would follow the stricter ruling of the House of Shammai and prohibit the use of demai citrons.

It can be imagined that a donkey can carry a load of several hundred citrons. Did Bar Kokhba intend that each soldier have their own four species? If so, then there must have been a few hundred rebels in Bar Kokhba's outpost. However, according to Jewish law, in times of need, many people can share the same four species. In the recent past, in Europe and America, an entire synagogue would share one or two sets of four species. If it was the intention of Bar Kokhba to have his faithful share the sets, then there must have been several thousand, and possibly 10,000 or more, troops at his head-quarters who required the species.

Another letter with regard to the same matter was also found, this one written in Greek. This letter does not contain the name of Shimon Bar Kokhba, and parts of the letter are missing.

> S...ios
> To Yehonathan . . . Be'ayan and Masabla
>
> . . . sending Agrippas so that they may send back the palms and citrons with him for the camp of the Jews.
> Be quick, do not delay. . . .
> . . . this letter is written in Greek as we have no one who knows Hebrew and the festival is approaching.
> Do not delay. Peace.[3]

It is not known if this letter was sent before or after the preceding letter. It is also not known from where or to where the letter was sent. Yadin supposes that Yehuda was not in Kiryat Arabaya when the first letter arrived. Yehuda placed S...ios in charge. S...ios dispatched Agrippas with a cover letter to Yehonathan and Masabla.

It seems that Yehuda had left the post in Kiryat Arabaya with all the Jewish soldiers, leaving only the non-Jews behind. That would explain why no one in the camp knew how to write Hebrew. Also, the fact that S...ios calls Bar Kokhba's camp the "camp of the Jews" indicates that it was a multinational force that joined in the rebellion. This is borne out by Dio Cassius, who wrote: "All Judea had been stirred up. Many other nations joined them for personal gain. The whole earth, one might say, was stirred up in the matter."[4]

Another letter, also written in Greek, which was poorly preserved, reads:

> Ailianos
> To brother Yonathes
>
> Peace.
> Simon Kosiba has written to me that you must send the
> . . . for the brothers' needs.
> [Ailia]nos
> Peace, my brothers.[5]

We do not know what Ailianos was requesting. Possibly it was another solicitation for the four species. Yadin points out the usage of the term *brother* among these revolutionaries, which is not unlike the modern-day term, *comrade*.

It is well known that in Hebrew only the consonants are written out, while the vowels are omitted. In Hebrew, Bar Kosiba's name is written *br ksb*. The first two letters, *br*, are very common; meaning *son of*, they are pronounced, "bar." However, the letters *ksb*, being a proper name and not found anywhere else, present a problem as to the exact pronunciation. However, in Greek, as in English, vowels are written out. In this letter, the name is written "Simon Kosiba." It is this fragment of a letter that gives us Shimon's exact family name.

12

The Cave

In late March 1960, the Israel Department of Antiquities and the Israel Exploration Society undertook a major two-week expedition in the Judean Desert, west of the Dead Sea. The area was dotted with hundreds, perhaps thousands, of caves. These caves had been raided and looted by the nomadic bedouins for scrolls to sell on the black market. Perhaps, the expedition leaders thought, some caves were untouched by these marauders.

One team of archaeologists, led by Y. Yadin, was charged with the area of Nahal Hever. This 2½-mile-long canyon is located between Ein Gedi and Masada. The almost vertical slopes rise upward almost 1,000 feet. Some scroll fragments had been found in this area seven years earlier.

On top of the northern precipice of the canyon were the remains of a Roman siege camp. It had a commanding view of the desert floor below and also of the caves of Nahal Hever. The camp was 160 feet long from east to west and 130 feet from north to south. About one hundred troops were stationed there. Any movement outside any of the caves could be detected and deterred by these Roman soldiers.

The particular cave that was the subject of the archaeologists' interest was located 300 feet below the precipice of the Roman camp. This 500-foot-long cavern, which is today inhabited by thousands of screeching bats, proved to be one of the most interesting, for it contained remains dating back to the Bar Kokhba rebellion.

On one of the first days of exploration, a startling and sobering discovery was made. In a niche of the cave was found a heap of baskets filled with skulls, but without the jaw bones. Nearby was another heap of baskets containing the remainders of the skeletons, together with the jaw bones. In all, the remains of three men, eight women, and six children were found. Then, a leather-lined basket containing the skeleton of a child wrapped in a tunic was uncovered. Subsequently, two more skeletons were found. It was later shown, by the discovery of letters and documents in the cave, that these were the remains of Jews who had sided with the legendary Shimon Bar Kokhba in his revolt against Rome.

How did these Jews meet their fate? Historical and talmudic sources relate how Roman battalions were set up along the main roads of Judea to capture and execute those who were sympathetic with the rebellion. Many Jews stayed off the roads and sought refuge in the mountain caves. These fleeing refugees had little or no food and starvation began to take its course. In desperation they had to feed upon the corpses of their fallen brothers.

The Midrash relates the following tale of horror:

One certain man had gone out each morning looking for a corpse to eat. One day he came across a body, the body of his father. He buried his father and set a marker to indicate the site. When he returned to the cave, a friend asked what he had found that day. "Nothing," replied the first one. The friend decided he would go out to try his luck. He found the buried corpse and brought it back and cooked the remains. The friend

shared his meal with the first man who had brought back
nothing to eat. While they were eating the first man asked his
friend where he found the corpse, since he had looked earlier
and found nothing. The friend said that he found it buried with
a marker over the gravesite. The first man began to choke and
cried out, "Woe, woe to me. I have eaten from the flesh of my
father to keep alive."[1]

Such was the degradation to which these revolutionaries had
to subject themselves.

With the Roman camp stationed above and with a 700-foot
sheer drop to the desert below, undoubtedly these Jews had
starved to death. Who gathered the skeletons and placed them
in the baskets? We can only guess. Perhaps another group of
Jews, hiding in later years, happened upon the remains, gathered the bones, and gave them the best burial they could.

13

Bronze Jugs

Several days later, the expedition made another discovery. A large basket containing nineteen bronze items was found. It contained twelve jugs, one large "frying pan," a key, two large bowls, and three fire-pans. A fire-pan looks like a metal dustpan and was made to hold burning coals. There were two small metal plates in the corners of the pan near the handle in which incense was kept. The incense was sprinkled onto the coals and its fragrant odor would fill the room.

The fire-pan was often used as a traditional symbol of the Jewish People. In the Arch of Titus in Rome is a depiction of victorious Roman soldiers carrying the spoils of war that they captured in Judea. Among the spoils borne high are fire-pans, for the burning of incense was an integral part of the Temple service.

Throughout the Roman and Byzantine eras, the menorah, the fire-pan, the shofar, and the palm branch with a citron were often depicted in synagogue frescoes and mosaics.

The bronze items discovered in the cave were manufactured in Italy and were obviously captured by the Jews from Romans. The jugs and the frying pan had human figures carved

Plate 7 Bronze pitcher with rubbed-out image on handle.

on them representing motifs of pagan mythology. The images had been rubbed out, conforming with the Jewish law prohibiting the possession of carved human forms.

The items were tightly packed in a basket as if readied to be quickly transported elsewhere. Perhaps an escape was being planned, but as evident from the skeletons that were found, it was not carried out.

The rubbed-out images, together with the "four species" letters that were subsequently found in this cave, attest to the strict adherence to Jewish law by these revolutionaries, even during such a time of great duress (see Plate 7).

14

Blue Wool

One of the finds in the cave sent excited rumors throughout the orthodox Jewish community. Some wads of blue wool and partially formed tassels were discovered. Why should these be cause for excitement, you ask. I shall explain.

According to biblical law,[1] four-cornered garments worn by males are required to have fringes, or tassels, in each corner. These are called "tzitzis." The tzitzis has eight strands, which are twirled and knotted near the top where it is attached to the garment. The Torah dictates that there shall be a strand of blue wool in the tzitzis.

The Tosefta states that the blue coloring agent used in the dying of the wool had to be made from a sea creature called "chilazon."[2] The extract from the chilazon was added to other ingredients and boiled to produce the blue dye.

This blue dye was very rare and expensive, and a counterfeit dye manufactured from indigo began to appear on the ancient market. The Sages developed an intricate chemical test to determine if a dye lot was genuine.[3]

About a thousand years ago, the art of producing the blue dye was lost. The identity of the creature called chilazon was

forgotten. Not a single strand of genuine blue wool had ever been found in any archaeological dig, nor had anyy
ancient tzitzis been found in any "geniza," a storage place for worn religious books and items. The blue wool tzitzis were still in use during the Bar Kokhba revolution. Could it be that the expedition had discovered the first remains of this mysterious dye in the cave?

A sample of the blue wool was sent to New York for infrared spectrophotometry analysis by the Dexter Chemical Corporation. The results were most disappointing. The test showed that the coloring agent was a combination of indigo and carminic acid. The blue wool was a fake.

Could it be that these traditional Jews who inhabited the cave almost two thousand years ago were duped? When I first saw the photographs of the partially formed tzitzis, two things caught my eye immediately. One, the tassels consisted entirely of blue wool, while according to the ritual law, part of the tassel had to consist of white wool. Second, it appeared as though the tassel was in the process of being twirled and knotted, to be later attached to the garment. However, according to ritual law, the tzitzis had to be twirled and knotted after the strands were set into the garment. Clearly, these tassels were never intended to be tzitzis but were merely decorative.

It does strike me as curious that no tzitzis were found in the cave. Several remnants of tunics were found, yet there was no tzitzis among them. It is quite possible that the inhabitants of the cave were Essene Jews, whose religious lore differed from the traditional rituals of the rabbinic Pharisees.

The Midrash (Tanchumah, Shelach) says: "Where is there a mitzva to use blue strands and white strands? When the blue strands are found. But now that the blue strands are *hidden*, the mitzva is performed only with white strands."

The Midrash says "the blue strands are hidden from us" — hidden, perhaps, somewhere in that cave.

15

The Essenes

A few miles east of Herodium, near the northwestern shore of the Dead Sea, is the desert city of Qumran (see Plate 8). Based on the discovery of Bar Kokhba coins in the ruins of Qumran, it is assumed that there was some relationship between the inhabitants of Qumran and the Bar Kokhba revolutionaries. Before we can attempt to guess at that relationship, we must know something about the mysterious inhabitants of this desert city.

Qumran's fame rests with the discovery of the so-called Dead Sea Scrolls, which were found in the caves nearby. Many scholars believe that the scrolls were written in this isolated desert town by the Jewish sect who inhabited the area, the Essenes.

One of the primary sources used in identifying Qumran with the sect of the Essenes is the first-century C.E. Roman historian, Pliny the Elder. In his *Naturalis Historia*, he writes:

On the west side of the Dead Sea, but out of range of the noxious vapors of the coast, is the solitary tribe of the Essenes, which is remarkable beyond all other tribes in the world. It has

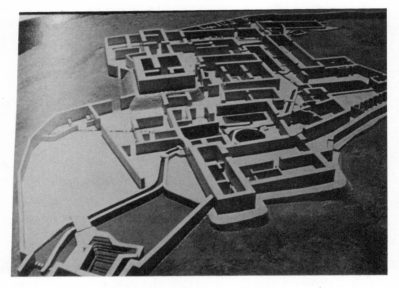

Plate 8 Archaeological model of Qumran.

no women, has renounced all sexual desire, has no money, and has only the palm trees for company. Day by day the throng of refugees is recruited. People tired of life are driven there by ways of fortune to adopt their manners.

Thus, through thousands of ages, a race in which no one is born lives on forever. So prolific, for their advantage is other men's weariness of life.

Below the Essenes was the former town of Ein Gedi, second only to Jerusalem in fertility of its land and in its growths of palm trees, but now like Jerusalem, a heap of ashes. Next comes Masada, a fortress on a rock, itself not far from the Dead Sea.[1]

Pliny's geographical location of the Essene community, west of the Dead Sea and above Ein Gedi, fits perfectly with Qumran.

The Essene sect of Jews had an admired religious dedication to their principles of purity and piety. Josephus Flavius, the first-century C.E. Jewish historian and contemporary of the sect, writes:

> The Essenes are known for their extreme piety and saintliness. They show greater mutual respect than do other sects. They hold pleasure to be a vice and temperance to be a virtue. They disdain marriage but adopt other people's children while young, molding them in their ways. They do not condemn marriage in principle, but desire to protect themselves against women's unfaithfulness.
>
> They hold wealth in contempt. All new members must surrender their property so that no poverty nor wealth can be seen. Each man's possessions become part of the group's resources.
>
> They regard perfumes as polluting. They all wear white. They choose officers to supervise the community affairs. The responsibility of each officer is decided by vote.
>
> When followers arrive from elsewhere, they place their resources at the guest's disposal. They entertain the men, whom they had never known, as though they were the best of friends.
>
> When they travel, they carry no baggage, only weapons to ward off robbers. In every community one officer oversees that new arrivals have clothing and provisions. Clothing and shoes are not changed until they are worn out and tattered. Nothing is bought or sold amongst themselves, but everyone gives to those in need.
>
> Before sunrise no one utters a word regarding secular affairs. In prayer they beseech God to make Himself known. Afterwards, they engage in crafts for which they have a reputation. At the fifth hour they immerse themselves in cold water and put on their sacred garments and assemble in a hall. No one is allowed to enter except the initiated.
>
> Everyone takes his seat in silence. A baker serves them loaves of bread and a cook sets before each one a prepared food. The priest recites the blessing; none may eat before the blessing. The meal begins with a blessing and commences with a blessing, giving honor to God as the bestower of life. They remove their sacred garments and return to work.

When they return in the evening, they resume eating in the same manner as before. The serving of meat and wine is curtailed. They speak softly, each in his turn. To outsiders, the softness of tones seems like some awesome mystery.

Giving of presents is forbidden unless approved by an elder. They keep tempers under control. Every word they utter is as binding as an oath. They are devoted to the study of ancient writings, mostly those that benefit the body and soul. They search out medicinal roots and healing stones.

Men convicted of major offenses are expelled from the order. They are bound by oath not to seek assistance elsewhere. They are reduced to eating grass and weeds. Eventually the body wastes and dies of starvation. Many offenders have been taken back at their last gasp for breath. They feel that any man who suffers to the point of death has sufficiently paid for his misdeeds.

They are just and scrupulous in trying court cases. Sentence is never passed in a tribunal of less than one hundred judges. After God, they hold Moses in great esteem. Whoever curses the name of Moses is sentenced to death. With regards to the Sabbath they are stricter than all Jews. They move no vessel on the holy day nor do they relieve themselves.[2]

From the Josephus description it appears that the Essenes were a highly spiritual people and would seem likely candidates to become followers of the long-awaited Messiah. But further analysis will show that this was not very likely.

In order to suppose that the Essenes and Bar Kokhba were spiritually akin, they would have to regard themselves as belonging to the same religion. In order for them to be coreligionists, they would have to share the same Bible and the same calendar. However, this was not the case, as I shall explain.

Historical and archaeological evidence indicates that the Essenes were dedicated to the study and copying of ancient texts. The texts that comprise the body of the traditional Jewish Bible were established by the Great Assembly around the fourth century B.C.E. This was accepted as law by the rabbinical community known as the Pharisees. However, the Essenes did not regard the word of the assembly as binding. Some of the Essene texts duplicated the text of the Pharisees and some of their texts differed. In addition, the Essenes had books that they regarded as sacred and the Pharisees deemed secular. The mere fact that the Pharisees and Essenes had two different Bibles would give rise to mutual suspicion between the two groups.

Perhaps the most noticeable difference between the Essene community and the Pharisees was in their respective calendars, which is the subject of our next chapter.

16

The Time of the Essenes

Time: its very essence has eluded philosophers and scientific theorists since the very beginning. What is this thing called time that is measured in seconds, minutes, hours, days, weeks, months, years, centuries, and millennia? Great thinkers from Aristotle to Albert Einstein have spent time pondering the very time they were contemplating. The passage of time is common to all creatures and creations. The creation of time is alluded to in the very first word of the Torah—"berayshis," meaning in the beginning of time, for creation could not exist without time; and, like creation itself, the mystery of time has eluded us.

Though man has no firm grasp as to the nature of time, still he can measure it. Lifetimes are measured in units of time. Daily appointments are set according to time. Hardly an hour goes by without checking the clock, to remind ourselves of the constant and irreversible forward flow of time. We wear a watch around the pulse site of the wrist because time is inextricably bound to the rhythmic pulse of life.

Religion gives meaning and purpose to life and the passage of time. It is no wonder that every religion has devised its own unique system of marking time, called the calendar. A religious sect would devise its own calendar to demonstrate its independence and defiance of other religious philosophies. Today, all branches of Judaism, even Conservative and Reform, use the same calendar to indicate their desire to be identified with normative Judaism. But this was not always the case with Jewish sects.

During the Second Temple Era and the years immediately thereafter, there were several renegade cults: the Essenes, the Saducees, and the Boetosees. The origin of the Essenes is not known, but the origin of the Saducees and Boetosees is recorded in the Midrash. The Sage Antignos of Socho advised his students, "Be not like the servants who attend the master in order to receive a reward."[1] Two of Antignos's disciples, Saduck and Boetose, misunderstanding their master, assumed he was indicating that there is no reward in the World to Come and in the Resurrection of the Dead. Thereupon they rejected the Oral Law and founded two apostate sects called the Sadducee and the Boetosee.

The exact distinction between these two sects is obscure. According to most scholars, the philosophies of these two denominations were identical. Both sects rejected the Oral Law and adhered to a strict literal exposition of Torah Law. The biblical injunction of "an eye for an eye" was interpreted to mean that the offender's eye should be gouged out. They both rejected the tradition of "Halacha from Moses on Sinai." In short, they outrightly rejected the traditions, the authority, and the interpretation of the Sages, whom they referred to as the Pharisees.

Since the religious philosophies of the Saducee and Boetosee sects seem to have been synonymous and since the contemporary writers, such as Philo and Josephus, only mention the Sadducees, we shall heretofore likewise include both sects under this name.

During the later part of the Second Temple Era, the Sadducees had gained great political and religious power. Sadducee priests had infiltrated the Temple service with their deviant practices. They mocked the Water-Drawing Ceremony on Succos that was held so dear by the traditional Jews. The Sadducees even became High Priests and corrupted the sacred incense offering that was offered on Yom Kippur in the Holy of Holies. The Sadducees established their own civil courts and yielded great influence over the reigning monarch.

The very first commandment given to the Children of Israel in Egypt was to establish a calendar. The calendar was to consist of twelve months. Each month would begin when witnesses attested to the appearance of the new moon. Each month would consist of twenty-nine or thirty days, depending on the sighting and the arrival of the witnesses and on the official proclamation of the court. At the discretion of the Sanhedrin, the witnesses could be held off one day and the proclamation of the new month could be postponed. The very foundation of the Jewish calendar and Jewish life rested with the authority of the Sages and the Sanhedrin.

The Mishna records that the practice of the Sanhedrin was to light bonfires to signal the onset of the newly proclaimed month.[2] When the Sadducees began to light their own bonfires to confuse the people, the Sanhedrin abolished the practice of lighting fires as a signal and instead sent runners to announce the new month.

The question to be raised concerns what motivated the Sadducees to disrupt the calendar. Would it not also cause confusion among their own members? The Sadducees, as mentioned earlier, had rejected the jurisdiction of the Sages, and they therefore had to construct a new calendar, one that was permanently set and did not hinge on the judicial discretion of rabbinical authorities.

It is known from various Essene Dead Sea Scrolls and certain pseudepigraphic writings, such as the Book of Jubilees and the Book of Enoch, that there was in existence during the mishnaic era another calendar, one that was used by the three renegade Jewish sects. That calendar consisted of 364 days and was based on the sun's revolution, not that of the moon. The sun, unlike the moon, does not go through phases. There is no appearance of a "new sun." Thus, the testimony of witnesses and judicial rulings would not be required.

The Book of Jubilees (2:9) says, "The sun shall be a great sign on the earth for days and for Sabbaths, for months and for festivals, for years and for the seasons of the year. . . . [C]ommand thou the Children of Israel that they observe the year according to this reckoning, three hundred and ssxty-four days, and these will constitute a complete year."

The 364-day solar calendar also consisted of twelve months. Each month had thirty days, except the third, sixth, ninth, and twelfth months, which had thirty-one. The uniqueness of this calendar is that if the year begins on Sunday, it will end on Saturday and the next year will again begin on Sunday. The calendar holidays will always fall out on the same day of the week, year after year.

The critical question is, on what day of the week did that calendar year begin? There are three logical choices. Either the year began on Sunday, the day the heavens and earth were created; it began on Wednesday, the day the sun was created; or it began on Friday, the day Man was created. Because of the unique structure of the Essene-Saducee calendar, if we only knew on which day of the week one Hebrew date occurred, we could reconstruct the entire yearly calendar. Now all we need is the day of the week for one date. Our search begins.

The Torah states: "In the first month, on the fourteenth day in the evening, is a Passover to God. On the fifteenth day of this month is the holiday of matzos . . . and you shall count for yourselves from the morrow of the Sabbath . . . seven weeks."[3] The Pharisee sages interpret the word *Sabbath* to refer to the first day of Passover. Labor is forbidden on that day, and the biblical term for such a day is Sabbath. The Torah is stating that the counting will begin on the day after that

Sabbath, namely, the second day of Passover. Fifty days later will be the festival of Shevuos.

The Sadducees and Essenes had a different interpretation. They took the phrase, "morrow of the Sabbath" to mean literally the day after the Saturday, meaning Sunday. The counting was to begin the first Sunday after the holiday of the matzos. Accordingly, Shevuos would arrive fifty days later, which would also be on Sunday.

On the first day of the counting, an omer measure of the new barley crop was harvested and brought as a meal offering in the Temple.

On the fiftieth day, Shevuos, a meal offering consisting of the new wheat crop was offered. The Pharisee sages maintained that the barley offering was on the second day of Passover, whereas the Sadducees and Essenes maintained that it was offered on the first Sunday after Passover. Both groups agreed that the wheat offering was performed fifty days after the barley offering.

In 1967, the Israeli government acquired a Dead Sea Scroll called the Temple Scroll. Its name is derived from the detailed description that the scroll devotes to the Messianic Temple. This Essene scroll does not conform to the prophetic description of Ezekiel, nor does it follow the halacha of the Talmud; but it does shed some interesting light on the subject of the Essenes' calendar and celebrations.

The Temple Scroll adheres to the Sadducee-Essene interpretation that the counting shall begin on the first Sunday after the first day of Passover. After mentioning the festival of Shevuos, the scroll continues to record two holidays that are not found in our traditional rabbinical literature.

The first holiday was called the Feast of the New Wine and was to be celebrated fifty days after Shevuos. "And you shall count from [Shevuos] day . . . seven weeks. . . . [T]he morrow of the seventh Sabbath you shall offer new wine as a drink offering . . . and they shall offer with the wine that day to the Lord twelve rams."

The second holiday was called the Feast of the New Oil and was to be celebrated fifty days after the Feast of the New Wine. "And you shall count from that day seven weeks. . . . [T]hen you shall offer new oil . . . on the altar of the burnt offering."

In the 1890s, a fragment of a book written by Saadiah Gaon (882–942), head of the religious community in Sura, Babylonia, was discovered in the Ezra Synagogue geniza in Old Cairo, Egypt. Saadiah Gaon records information concerning the aberrant Karaite calendar. The Karaites were the later-day successors of the Sadducees. Saadiah Gaon writes:

> Just as there are fifty days between the first fruits of barley [offered on "the morrow of the Sabbath"] and the first fruits of wheat [offered on Shevuos], so there are fifty days between the first fruits of wheat and the first fruits of wine . . . and between the first fruits of the wine and the first fruits of the oil are fifty days. The oil offering falls on the twentieth of Elul."[4]

We know that the Sadducee-Essene Shevuos always fell on a Sunday. Fifty days later was the Feast of the New Wine, also on a Sunday, and fifty days after that was the Feast of New Oil, also on a Sunday. Saadiah Gaon states that the date of the Sunday of the New Oil feast was 20 Elul. Based on this one date, Sunday the twentieth of Elul, we can reconstruct the entire Sadducee calendar and can determine that their year began on Friday, the day when Adam and Eve were created (see Plate 9).

To show their rejection of rabbinical Judaism, the Sadducees had created their own calendar. To flaunt their disregard for the Sages, they lit bonfires to confuse the traditionalist Jews. This confusion would in no way disrupt their own set calendar.

1   N I S A N

S	M	T	W	TH	F	SA
					1	2
3	4	5	6	7	8	9
10	11	12	13	14	15	16
17	18	19	20	21	22	23
24	25	26	27	28	29	30

2   I Y A R

S	M	T	W	TH	F	SA
1	2	3	4	5	6	7
8	9	10	11	12	13	14
15	16	17	18	19	20	21
22	23	24	25	26	27	28
29	30					

3   S I V A N

S	M	T	W	TH	F	SA
		1	2	3	4	5
6	7	8	9	10	11	12
13	14	15	16	17	18	19
20	21	22	23	24	25	26
27	28	29	30	31		

4   T A M U Z

S	M	T	W	TH	F	SA
					1	2
3	4	5	6	7	8	9
10	11	12	13	14	15	16
17	18	19	20	21	22	23
24	25	26	27	28	29	30

5   A V

S	M	T	W	TH	F	SA
1	2	3	4	5	6	7
8	9	10	11	12	13	14
15	16	17	18	19	20	21
22	23	24	25	26	27	28
29	30					

6   E L U L

S	M	T	W	TH	F	SA
		1	2	3	4	5
6	7	8	9	10	11	12
13	14	15	16	17	18	19
20	21	22	23	24	25	26
27	28	29	30	31		

7-   T I S H R E

S	M	T	W	TH	F	SA
					1	2
3	4	5	6	7	8	9
10	11	12	13	14	15	16
17	18	19	20	21	22	23
24	25	26	27	28	29	30

8-   C H E S H V

S	M	T	W	TH	F	SA
1	2	3	4	5	6	7
8	9	10	11	12	13	14
15	16	17	18	19	20	21
22	23	24	25	26	27	28
29	30					

9-   K I S L E V

S	M	T	W	TH	F	SA
		1	2	3	4	5
6	7	8	9	10	11	12
13	14	15	16	17	18	19
20	21	22	23	24	25	26
27	28	29	30	31		

10   T E V E S

S	M	T	W	TH	F	SA
					1	2
3	4	5	6	7	8	9
10	11	12	13	14	15	16
17	18	19	20	21	22	23
24	25	26	27	28	29	30

11   S H V A T

S	M	T	W	TH	F	SA
1	2	3	4	5	6	7
8	9	10	11	12	13	14
15	16	17	18	19	20	21
22	23	24	25	26	27	28
29	30					

12   A D A R

S	M	T	W	TH	F	SA
		1	2	3	4	5
6	7	8	9	10	11	12
13	14	15	16	17	18	19
20	21	22	23	24	25	26
27	28	29	30	31		

Plate 9 The Essene Calendar.

The Jerusalem Talmud records that the Sadducees once hired false witnesses to testify that the new moon of Nissan appeared on a Saturday.[5] Their motive was to cause the first day of Passover to fall on a Saturday so that Shevuos would occur on Sunday, which was their tradition. The commentaries wonder why the Sadducees were not concerned about the distortion of the proper date of Passover that would result due to the false testimony. The solution is that the Sadducees had their own, solar-based calendar, which would be unaffected by either the correct or the incorrect testimony of witnesses.

In light of the above we can more fully appreciate the enormous religious strife and conflict that existed in the Mishnaic Era. Many sections of the Talmud are devoted to disproving various contentions and beliefs of the Sadducees. But the ultimate struggle was for the supremacy of the calendar, for the battle over the calendar is the struggle for time, and the struggle for time is the struggle for life and its meaning.

As mentioned in the preceding chapter, the discovery of Bar Kokhba coins in the Essene community of Qumran indicates some sort of relationship between the two groups. Whatever that relationship was, it was not one of mutual respect and admiration. Bar Kokhba was the proclaimed Messiah, attested to by the Pharisee leader, Rabbi Akiva. The Essenes, with their own traditions, Bible, and calendar, could not philosophically acknowledge the proclamation of a Pharisee Messiah. Were the Essenes a sect conquered by Bar Kokhba? Did they voluntarily submit to his rule because of their mutual hatred of the Roman enemy? Whatever the association was between these two opposing sects, we do not know. However, one of the Essene Dead Sea Scrolls may have a bearing on the messianic movement, and that is the Messiah Fragment.

17

The Messiah Fragment

A tiny fragment of a Dead Sea scroll has lately come into the spotlight (see Plate 10). It is only 1½ by 2 inches and has been given the catchy name of 4Q285—meaning Qumran cave number 4, fragment 285. The text contains only seventeen words on a few lines. The rest of the scroll has not been found. The top, bottom, left side, and right side of the fragment are missing. Called the Messiah Fragment, it has been translated by Professor Robert Eisenman of California State University, Professor Michael Wise of the University of Chicago, and Professor Emeritus Geza Vermes of Oxford University. The fragment reads as follows. (Since the translators do not always agree as to the identification and translation of a word, I have put the initial letter of the last name of the translator I am using at the end of the line.)

> . . . Isaiah the prophet . . . (E,W,V)
> . . . the scepter shall go forth from the root of Jesse . . . (E,W)
> . . . the branch of David . . . (E,W,V)
> . . . and they shall enter into judgment . . . (V)

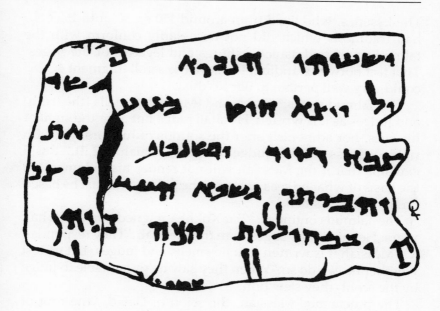

Plate 10 The Messiah Fragment.

. . . and they shall put to death the prince, the branch of
David . . . (E,W)
. . . with wounds and the priest shall order . . . (E,W,V)

The fragmentary bit of information contained in the parchment tells of the Prophet Isaiah prophetically describing the Messianic Era. ("The scepter shall go forth from the root of Jesse" refers to the messianic descendant of King David, the son of Jesse.) Someone will sit in judgment against the Messiah, and the judges will have him killed. It is no wonder that this small bit of parchment has captivated some Christian scholars, who believe it may refer to the death sentence imposed on Jesus.

Many of the Dead Sea Scrolls are termed "pesharim," or interpretations, and were written by the Essene sect of Jews.

The Essenes, who lived from around 150 B.C.E. until 150 C.E., had traditions which did not necessarily conform with the talmudic and midrashic teachings and legacies of the Sages. That fact notwithstanding, I believe the scroll fragment 4Q285 could very well pertain to Bar Kokhba.

The Talmud states:[1] "Raba said [Messiah] smells [the truth] and judges as it is written 'He shall judge not after the sight of his eyes, nor admonish after the sounds of his ears, yet with righteousness shall he judge the poor' (Isaiah 11:2,3)." Rashi explains that if the Messiah will not render his judgment on the basis of what he sees or hears, the judgment must be based on his sense of smell.[2]

The Talmud continues: "Bar Kokhba reigned two and a half years. He said to the Sages 'I am the Messiah.' They responded 'Of Messiah it is written that he smells and judges. Let us test whether he can do so.' When they saw he was unable to judge by the scent, they slew him."[3]

The proclaimed Messiah, the scion of David, "the root of Jesse," was judged to be false "and they put to death the prince, the branch of David."[4] Could it be that fragment 4Q285 was the Essenes' way of recording the death of Bar Kokhba and disguising it in the form of a prophecy of Isaiah? We cannot tell for certain. Perhaps when dating tests are performed on the fragment, some light will be shed.

An interesting footnote on this matter is that the second line of the fragment, "the scepter shall go forth from the root of Jesse," is a verbatim quote from Isaiah 11:1. The talmudic tradition that the Messiah could smell truth is based on the very next two verses of Isaiah, 11:2 and 11:3.

It is also intriguing to speculate if this Essene fragment is gleefully "foretelling" the downfall of the Pharisee Messiah, Bar Kokhba.

18

The Bar Kokhba Temple

In his monumental code of law, Maimonides states that a primary function of the Messiah is to build the Third Temple, as described in the book of Ezekiel.[1] Bar Kokhba firmly believed that he was the Messiah. He had confirmation from the greatest rabbis of his generation. Surely Bar Kokhba should have made the rebuilding of the Temple a priority objective.

It is my contention that there certainly exists the possibility that Bar Kokhba did, in fact, build a Third Temple. Though there is no clear record of such a historical event, I believe that there are enough clues and indications in the Talmud, Midrash, ancient secular writings, and archaeological remains to warrant an exploration of the matter.

1. By Torah law, the sacrificial Pascal lamb had to be roasted directly over a fire. The question was raised in the Talmud if the use of a metal grill to support the roasting animal was permitted.[2] Would the entire meat be roasted directly from the heat of the fire or would some of the meat be seared from the heat absorbed by the metal grill?

The Talmud offers support that a metal grill is permissible, from the fact that Rabban Gamliel ordered his servant to grill the Pascal sacrifice over a metal grill.

Rabban Gamliel was the grandfather of Rabbi Judah the Prince, the compiler of the Mishna. Rabbi Judah was born the same day Rebbe Akiva died, circa 135 C.E. From the context of the talmudic passage, it seems that Rabban Gamliel was an established authority at the time when he ordered his servant to grill the Pascal sacrifice, and therefore, evidence could be offered based on his actions. Let us assume that the youngest that Rabban Gamliel could have been at the time of the sacrificial offering was twenty-five.

If the offering was done in the Second Temple, which was destroyed in 70 C.E. — and let us assume it was offered in the last possible year — that means that Rabban Gamliel was born in the year 45 C.E., at the very latest. That would make, at the very least, a ninety-year difference in age between grandfather and grandson. This is unlikely, since the grandson was the firstborn and the son of a firstborn and since the Sages married at a very early age.

It makes more sense to assume that Rabban Gamliel was born later than 45 C.E. and that he offered his sacrifice after the destruction of the Second Temple. Where did he offer it? In the Bar Kokhba Temple.

One of the nineteenth-century talmudic commentaries, by Rabbi Shmuel Shtrashun of Vilna, also offers this as a possible solution to the problem of Rabban Gamliel's age.[3] However, he is perturbed by the lack of confirmation in talmudic literature as to the building of a Bar Kokhba Temple.

2. Bar Kokhba issued coins when he recaptured Judea. These coins are mentioned in the Talmud.[4] Some of these coins depicted the facade of the Holy Temple. It was a common practice among the nations of those times to picture a temple on coins; but it was never the practice to depict a nonexisting building on a coin. This would be meaningless to the people.

Plate 11 The Temple facade as depicted on a Bar Kokhba coin.

Bar Kokhba's Temple facade had to have been a representation of an existing building (see Plate 11).

3. In the 1930s, archaeological excavations in Dura-Europos, Syria, uncovered an ancient synagogue, which was constructed aroun

showing the Temple. The resemblance to the facade depicted on the Bar Kokhba coins is remarkable. Both show exactly the same doorway, a curved arch with double doors. Both show four columns in front of the doorway supporting a roof. Both show a scalloped edging on top of the roof. From where did the Dura-Europos builders get this image? If it was from the Bar Kokhba coins, then the images should have been exactly the same. But, there are some differences. The Bar Kokhba coins show columns with Doric-style capitals, whereas the fresco has Corinthian-style capitals. The fresco also shows two columns flanking the doorway. The coins do not show these two columns because the image on the coin is too small to accommodate this detail (see Plate 12).

If the painters of the fresco were not copying the Bar Kokhba coins, from where did they get the image? One theory offered is that they copied the Temple to Jupiter, built by Hadrian, that stood atop the Temple Mount. But why would Jews use a picture of a pagan temple to beautify their synagogue? I believe that a better explanation is that Bar Kokhba built a Temple on the Temple Mount. When Hadrian later recaptured Jerusalem, he did not tear down the Bar Kokhba Temple and build his temple to Jupiter. Hadrian simply converted the Bar Kokhba Temple into a pagan temple.

Thus, the Dura-Europos artists were copying the image of a Temple that still stood when the fresco was commissioned.

4. On some of the Bar Kokhba coins is the name of Bar Kokhba's High Priest, Elazer. Why would Bar Kokhba appoint a High Priest if there was no Temple, since the primary function of the high priest was to officiate in the Temple service on Yom Kipper? The most obvious answer is that indeed there was a Temple.

5. The Talmud records:

It once happened that Rabban Gamliel was sitting on a step on the Temple Mount and standing before him was the scribe Yochanan. . . . [Rabban Gamliel] asked him to write a letter "To our brethren in exile in Babylonia, our brethren in Media, and the rest of our brethren in exile. May your peace be ever great. We wish to inform you that the doves are immature, and the lambs are too young, and that the spring season has not reached. The thing appears proper to me and my colleagues that thirty days should be added to the year."[5]

Plate 12 The Dura-Europos fresco.

The traditional commentaries explain that Rabban Gamliel was concerned that Passover festival should not occur too early that year. The newborn doves and lambs would not reach the required age of maturity to be acceptable as sacrificial animals in the Temple service. It was, therefore, decided to proclaim a leap year, adding another month to the calendar in order to give the birds and lambs an additional thirty days to mature.

According to Rashi, Tosfos, and Rabbaynu Chananel, this incident occurred after Rabban Gamliel had been deposed as head of the academy in Yaveneh, which explains why he was in Jerusalem. Rabban Gamliel was deposed many years after the destruction of the Second Temple, and yet, he was concerned about having a sufficient supply of qualified sacrificial animals. That seems to indicate there was a Temple and

Temple service after the Second Temple had been destroyed—another indication of a Third Temple.

To be sure, Rabbaynu Nissim (Rahn) suggests that though there was no standing Temple at the time of the incident, Rabban Gamliel was concerned about the possibility that the Messiah would come shortly. Should he quickly rebuild the Temple, there would be an insufficient supply of qualified sacrificial animals.

Rabbaynu Nissim was certainly bothered by the dilemma I present here. I leave it to the talmudic scholars to decide whose solution is the more probable.

6. In the Talmud Rebbe Oshiyah says, "[The Sages] wanted to prohibit the use of all silver and gold because it may have come from the silver and gold in Jerusalem [which was sacred]." But, the Talmud continues, we asked him, "Does Jerusalem account for most of the silver and gold in the world?" (Why prohibit all silver and gold because of the slight possibility it may have come from the sacred treasures of Jerusalem?) He answered, "They only thought to prohibit the old Trajianic Hadrianic coins [whiih were minted from the silver and gold from the Temple treasury]."[6]

The Talmud is saying that the bullion used in Roman coins issued under the emperor Hadrian was taken from the Temple. Rashi comments that the captured silver was from the half-shekel coins pledged by the Israelites every year to purchase animals for public sacrifices.

It is the accepted understanding that after the destruction of the Second Temple there were no more sacrifices, either public or private. There was no longer any requirement to donate the half-shekel for the public offerings. Why would the Talmud think that during the reign of Hadrian, sixty years after the destruction, there would still be sacred coins?

Bar Kokhba ruled during the Hadrianic era. If Bar Kokhba did build a Temple, it is understood that the half-shekel donations would be reinstituted. When Hadrian subsequently captured Jerusalem and the Temple, he plundered the sacred Temple treasury.

The Talmud referred to the coins as Trajianic Hadrianic coins. Rashi explains this to mean the silver coins of the emperors Trajan and Hadrian. Later, in chapters 21 and 22, we shall see that Bar Kokhba first led a successful rebellion, called the Second Revolt, under the rule of the emperor Trajan. It was during this period that Bar Kokhba would have built his Third Temple.

The rebellion was temporarily quashed. Trajan recaptured Jerusalem and sacked the Temple treasury. A few years later, a second Bar Kokhba uprising, called the Third Revolt, occurred under the rule of Hadrian. The Temple service once again came to life. However, Hadrian put an end to the Bar Kokhba rebellion and ended the messianic hopes of the Jews. He, too, looted the Temple treasury. Any half-shekel coins donated to a Bar Kokhba Temple would be coins from the Trajianic and Hadrianic reigns. These sacred coins were despoiled by the Romans, and it was these coins that the Sages sought to prohibit.

7. During the early part of the common era, there was a group of secular Jewish poets. Their works were collected in a series of books entitled the *Sibylinne Oracles*. One of the poems, which was composed during the reign of Hadrian, refers to a great savior who built a "house" (temple) to God. The parenthetical comments are mine.

> For there came from the heavenly plain a man
> One blessed, with scepter in hand [Bar Kokhba, the divinely
>   appointed king]
> Which God gave him, and he ruled all things well
> And unto all the good did he restore
> The riches which the earlier men had seized
> And many cities with much fire he took [from the Romans]
> From their foundations, and he set on fire

The towers of mortals who before did evil
And he made that city which God loved [Jerusalem]
More radiant than stars and sun and moon
And he set order and a holy house [Temple]
Incarnate made, pure, very fair, and formed
In many stades a great and boundless tower
Touching the clouds themselves and seen by all
So that all holy and righteous men
Might see the glory of the eternal God
A sight that has been longed for. Rising sun
And setting day hymned forth the praise of God
For there are then no longer fearful things
For wretched mortals, nor adulteries
And lawless love of boys, nor homicide
Nor tumult, but a righteous strife in all
It is the last time of the saints when God
Accomplished these things, high thunderer
Founder of the temple most magnificent [emphasis mine].[7]

Another, similar poem, written by a Jewish Alexandrian
Sibylinne poet, reads:

Dear Jewish land! fair town, inspired of songs,
No more shall unclean foot of Greeks within they bounds go
    forth . . .,

For from the heavenly land a happy man comes forth,
Within whose hand a scepter given by God . . .,

The towns by fire leveled to the very earth,
And burnt the homes of men who once did evil,
But the town of beloved of God he made
Brighter than stars or sun and than the moon,
Adorned them brightly, and reared a holy Temple.

Modern scholars have pondered about the meaning of these
poems. They make reference to a heavenly inspired king who
recaptured the land, abolished the social evils, and founded a

new Temple. It is known that the poem was written during the years of the Hadrianic rule. Out of desperation, some scholars, such as Heinrich Graetz, suggested that these secular Jews were actually praising Hadrian. I think it more plausible that they were recording the successes of Bar Kokhba and his rebuilding of the Temple.

8. The Midrash states: "When Hadrian entered the Holy of Holies, he showed great arrogance and blasphemed God."[8]

How could Hadrian enter the Holy of Holies? Wasn't the Second Temple destroyed more than sixty years earlier by Titus? Perhaps, however, Hadrian entered the Holy of Holies of Bar Kokhba's Third Temple.

9. A similar piece of evidence can be derived from another Midrash: "Hadrian, may his bones be turned to dust, came and dashed the Temple stones."[9]

10. The seventh-century Byzantine historian known as Chronicum Paschale, drawing upon earlier records, writes: "Hadrian tore down the Temple of the Jews in Jerusalem and built two public baths, a theatre, and the Temple of Jupiter."[10]

11. An animal with a hole in the esophagus or other vital organ is unkosher. Generally speaking, animals were examined after slaughtering to ascertain if there were any internal defects that would render its meat unkosher. The Talmud states that one may eat the meat of the examined animal even though there is a remote possibility that the slaughtering knife passed through a hole in the esophagus, which would now be undetectable.[11] The principle is that we assumed the more probable circumstance, namely, that there was no puncture in the esophagus to begin with.

The Talmud asks, concerning Rebbe Meir's view, that since we do consider even remote possibilities, how could he permit meat to be eaten? The Talmud suggests that perhaps he forbade all meat. The Talmud asks further, would Rebbe Meir also prohibit sacrificial meat, such as the Pascal lamb, which was a mitzva, to be consumed?

Rashi, explaining the question, says, "Would Rebbe Meir prohibit sacrificial meat? Surely Rebbe Meir ate [from the Pascal lamb]."[12]

Rebbe Meir lived during the Hadrianic and Bar Kokhba era. Was there a Pascal Sacrifice then? An obvious conclusion is that there were sacrifices—sacrifices in the Bar Kokhba Temple.

12. Maimonides writes:

> Five things occurred on the Ninth of Av. [On that date] it was decreed upon the Israelites in the desert that they would not enter the land. The First and Second Temples were destroyed. A great city was conquered and Betar was its name. It was inhabited by thousands and tens of thousands of Jews. They had a great king who was accepted by the Jews and the great wise men as being the messianic king. It fell into Roman hands and they were all massacred. That tragedy equaled the destruction of the Temple. On that same day, which was destined for tragedy, the evil [governor] Tinnius Rufus plowed up the Temple Sanctuary and its environs.[13]

Maimonides states that the Roman governor during the Hadrianic persecution, Tinnius Rufus, plowed up the Temple. Which Temple is meant? The Second had been destroyed more than half a century earlier by Titus. Could Maimonides then be referring to the Bar Kokhba Temple?

13. The Talmud records an incident: "There was an Aramenean who went up to Jerusalem to eat of the Pascal sacrifice. He bragged that the Torah prohibits non-Jews and the uncircumcised from eating the sacrifice, and, yet, he eats from the very beet portion." The Talmud continues:

> Rebbe Yehuda ben Bisayra asked him if the Temple priests gave him the tail. The Aramenean answered, "They did not." Rebbe Yehuda ben Bisayra said that they do not give you the tail because they know you are not a Jew and the tail, which is the best part, is reserved for the Jews. The Aramenean did not

believe Rebbe Yehuda. The Rabbi said that when you go again, ask to be given the tail.

[The next year] when the Aramenean went to Jerusalem, he asked for the tail. The priests wondered, the tail is burnt upon the Altar [no one eats from it]. They asked the Aramenean as to who told him to ask for the tail. The Aramenean replied that Rebbe Yehuda ben Bisayra [told him].

Everyone was curious [that Rebbe Yehuda instructed him to ask for the tail]. They checked after him and discovered that he was an Aramenean and killed him.

The people sent a message to Rebbe Yehuda "Peace unto you, Rebbe Yehuda ben Bisayra. Though you are in Netzivon, your nets are spread in Jerusalem."[14]

Tosfos gets the distinct impression that Rebbe Yehuda ben Bisayra himself did not go up to Jerusalem to offer a Pascal sacrifice and wonders why.[15] One of the suggested answers is that Rebbe Yehuda was simply too old to travel.

When did this incident occur? Without giving the matter much thought, we would say that it took place sometime during the Second Temple Era. However, that is not possible. Rebbe Yehuda ben Bisayra was the legal authority after the death of Rebbe Akiva in 135 c.e. The Temple was destroyed in 70 c.e., and Tosfos says that Rebbe Yehuda was an old man at the time of the incident.

It could very well be that the incident took place in the Bar Kokhba Temple. Rebbe Yehuda was an old man at that time and yet could still survive Rebbe Akiva, who was murdered in 135 c.e., to become the next legal authority of the Jewish People.[16]

14. The Talmud records:

A man forbade to himself any pleasure from his wife should she make the festival pilgrimage. The wife went against his wishes and made the pilgrimage. The matter came before Rebbe Yossi. He said to the husband, "Had you known that she would have gone against your wishes and made the pilgrimage, would you have forbade upon yourself all pleasure from her?" He answered that he would not have. Rebbe Yossi then absolved him from the prohibition.[17]

Tosfos states that Rebbe Yossi was not born until after the Temple's destruction, and yet Rebbe Yossi ruled on a case that involved the Temple pilgrimage.[18] This indicates that there were pilgrimages and sacrifices after the year 70 c.e., when the Second Temple was destroyed.

The next piece of evidence is perhaps the most compelling and deserves a chapter of its own.

19

The Dome of the Rock

All the indications presented heretofore are based on literary works, both religious and secular. The next piece of evidence is based on archaeological remains and mathematical probability. It is perhaps the strongest argument for the case of a Bar Kokhba Third Temple.

Presiding over the Temple Mount today is the Moslem structure called the Dome of the Rock. This gold-domed building is built on an elevated platform. Evidence suggests, and archaeologists assume, that this elevated platform is some remnant of the Second Temple flooring (see Plate 13).

The platform is about 15¾ feet high. It is 550 feet from north to south and 540 feet from east to west.

In the Second Temple, there were two main floor levels. The larger area was the Temple Mount Courtyard and was 500 cubits by 500 cubits.[1] A cubit is approximately 1½ feet. Therefore, the Temple Mount Courtyard was 750 feet by 750 feet. The platform of the Dome is only 550 by 540 feet. It is too small to have been the flooring of the Temple Mount Courtyard.

The other floor level in the Second Temple was the elevated main courtyard, called the Azarah Courtyard. The Azarah

Plate 13 The Dome of the Rock and its platform, circa 1865.

Courtyard contained the Altar and the main Temple structure, the Sanctuary, which housed the Holy and the Holy of Holies. The Azarah Courtyard was 135 cubits by 187 cubits, or 202½ feet by 280½ feet.[2] The platform of the dome is much too large to have been the flooring of the Azarah Courtyard.

If the platform is too large to be the Azarah Courtyard and too small to be the Temple Mount Courtyard, what was it? The Third Temple, to be built by the Messiah, is described in the book of Ezekiel. It differs radically from the Second Temple, as described in the Tractate Midos. According to the commentary Tzuras HaBayis, written by Rabbi Yom Tov Lipman Heller, the Azarah Courtyard of the Messianic Temple is to be 346 cubits from north to south, and 340 cubits from east to west (about 519 feet by 510 feet). These figures approach the existing dome's platform dimensions of 550 by 540 feet.

But considering a cubit to be 1½ feet or 18 inches, is only an educated guess. What if the cubit is 19 inches or, more precisely, 19.07 inches? Then, the Messianic Azarah Courtyard of 346 cubits by 340 cubits would equal 550 feet by 540 feet, the precise dimensions of the platform of the dome!

The length and width of the prophetic Third Temple are 346 cubits and 340 cubits, forming a ratio (width divided by length) of approximately 1 to .9826589. The length and width of the dome's platform are 550 feet and 540 feet. That is a ration of 1 to .9818181. The difference between the two ratios is about .0008. Since the length of the platform is 550 feet, that equals 6,600 inches. A variable of .0008 of 6,600 inches would equal 5¼ inches.

The figures 550 and 540 feet are only approximate. There is a margin of error of about 2 or 3 feet. Since our difference was only 5.28 inches, the difference between the two ratios is negligible.

Although the two ratios are similar, we must demonstrate that they are one and the same. The cubit is known to be between 18 and 24 inches. In order for the two ratios to be, not only similar, but the very same, the one unit of measure, the cubit, must convert to the other unit, feet and inches, and fall between the narrow spectrum of 18 to 24 inches. It does, at 19.07 inches.

Either we have stumbled on one of the greatest of mathematical coincidences or we have found evidence of a Temple built according to the vision of Ezekiel.

According to Maimonides, the Azarah Courtyard is to be built on an elevated platform surrounded by a retaining wall 10 cubits high.[3] The platform of the dome is surrounded by a retaining wall and is about 15½ to 16 feet high. If the platform is the remains of the messianic Bar Kokhba Temple, and if a cubit is 19.07 inches, then the retaining wall of the dome platform is the very wall to which Maimonides refers. Ten cubits equals 15.89 feet, the approximate height of the present-day retaining wall.

20

Counterarguments

Four arguments are given by those who oppose the proposition of a Bar Kokhba Temple. One, there is no mention at all in any of the talmudic or midrashic sources of such a structure. Second, the Messianic Temple, according to early rabbinic commentaries, is supposed to be built by Divine miracle and not by man. Third, there is no indication that Bar Kokhba captured Jerusalem. Fourth, according to the talmudic sources, Bar Kokhba only ruled for two and a half years. That is not enough time to build a Temple. I shall address these arguments one at a time.

1. There is no mention at all in any of the talmudic or midrashic sources of such a structure.

It is true that there is no written source indicating that Bar Kokhba built a Temple. Why there is no mention, I shall not speculate. However, rabbinic commentaries and secular historians do mention the following story regarding the building of the Third Temple.

During the early part of the fourth century C.E., under Constantine the Great, the Roman Empire rejected paganism and assumed Christianity as the state religion. The seat of the empire was moved to Byzantium in Turkey. The Christians were the avowed foes of their brother Jews and, as in a bitter sibling rivalry, despised the Jews more than the pagan Romans. Oppressive taxes were levied upon the suffering Jews.

In November of 361, Julian became the emperor. He was raised a pagan and was taught tolerance by his teachers. He rejected the Christian religion but allowed religious freedom throughout the empire. It is no wonder the Jews regarded him as a savior and no wonder the Church branded him Julian the Apostate.

In a letter to his Jewish constituents, Julian wrote:

In the past, more oppressive to you than the yoke of dependence were the unjust taxes imposed upon you. You were compelled to furnish an immense quantity of gold to the imperial treasury. With my own hand I have thrown into the flames all past tax records so that even their memory shall not remain. I have placed my brother, the venerable Patriarch Julos, to see that no oppression is placed upon you. Everyone in my empire shall be free of care and enjoy peace to its fullest.

May you address your fervent prayers for my empire to the Almighty Creator of the Universe, who has supported me with His strong right arm.

. . . and upon the successful conclusion of the Persian War, I shall come to Jerusalem, the Holy City, which shall be rebuilt at my expense, for you have desired to see it restored these many years. I shall then join with you in offering praise to the Almighty.[1]

Julian appointed Alypius of Antioch to see that no expense was spared in restoring Jerusalem to its former glory. The governors of Syria and Judea were ordered to aid the cause in any way they could. Not only was the Holy City to be restored, but the Temple Mount was to be cleared of debris and a Temple was to be rebuilt.

The mountain was cleared and storehouses with supplies filled the ancient Jewish capital. Money from abroad was sent. Jewish women sold their jewelry and forwarded the funds.

The Christian citizens resented the newfound recognition of the Jews. The Christians rioted and in Edessa the entire Jewish population was killed. But the holy work continued. The building of the Temple structure began and, perhaps, was even completed, when a sudden earthquake rocked the mountain. Fires broke forth from beneath the foundations and destroyed all that had been done.

Shortly thereafter, all hopes of the Jewish community were dashed. During the Persian campaign, Julian was killed by one of his own soldiers, a Christian. A new emperor took the reins of the Byzantine Empire, Jovian the Christian.

This happened during the Talmudic Era. As mentioned earlier, it has been recorded by secular historians and Jewish commentaries (Seder HaDoros, Shalsheles HaKabbalah, Zemach Dovid, and Malbim at the conclusion to his commentary to Daniel). Yet no mention is made of this Third Temple on Mount Moriah in the Talmud or Midrash. Why is this? I do not know. But it does offer evidence of two things. Not every major historical event is recorded in the Talmud, and also, it is not a prerequisite for the Third Temple to be built by heavenly miracles.

2. The Messianic Temple, according to early rabbinic commentaries, is supposed to be built by Divine miracle and not by man.

Rashi and Tosfos mention that the Messianic Temple will be built by Heaven, implying it will not be built by man.[2] However, Maimonides, in his code of law, cites that there is a mitzva to build the Temple.[3] Maimonides only records mitzvos that either presently apply or will apply in the future days, as he himself writes in his Sefer HaMitzvos.[4] If the Temple is to be built by Divine miracle, what mitzva is involved? Also, if God is going to build that Temple, why was it necessary for all the dimensions of the Third Temple to be recorded in the book of Ezekiel? Obviously, there is a mitzva for the Jewish people to build that Temple. Minchas Chinuch also speculates that if conditions permit, it may be a required mitzva to build the Third Temple in our time.[5]

Is there then an argument between Rashi/Tosfos and Maimonides? There is not necessarily a disagreement. The great Lithuanian luminary, Rabbi Yosef Ber Solovetchic, in his magnum opus, *Bais HaLevi*, states that two possible scenarios are possible at the "end of days."[6] If the Jewish People merit it, great miracles will occur. Otherwise, the deliverance will take the form of a more natural occurrence.

Rashi and Tosfos are merely describing the possible miraculous end of days. Rashi and Tosfos are explaining how the Talmud could state that the Messiah could arrive late on the Eve of Succos and yet the Temple will be constructed before the Festival begins.[7] Obviously, the Talmud is considering a miraculous event. Maimonides, on the other hand, is citing the mitzva of rebuilding the Temple should the miracle not occur.

The fact that Rebbe Akiva would have allowed Bar Kokhba to build a Temple would not violate any principle of halacha.

3. There is no indication that Bar Kokhba captured Jerusalem.

There certainly is an indication that Jerusalem was captured. The Talmud states that one may not redeem the tithe with Jerusalemite Bar Kokhba coins.[8] What is meant by Jerusalemite Bar Kokhba coins? All the dozen or so different Bar Kokhba coins that have been found contain one of the following six inscriptions listed below.

1. YEAR 1 FREEDOM OF ISRAEL / SHIMON PRESIDENT OF ISRAEL
2. YEAR 2 FREEDOM OF ISRAEL / JERUSALEM

3. YEAR 2 FREEDOM OF ISRAEL / SHIMON
4. SHIMON / FREEDOM OF JERUSALEM
5. ELAZER THE PRIEST / FREEDOM OF JERUSALEM
6. SHIMON / ELAZER THE PRIEST

Three of the coins have the name *Jerusalem* on them. Those are the Jerusalemite Bar Kokhba coins to which the Talmud refers. Inscriptions 4 and 5 proclaim that Jerusalem was liberated from Roman dominion.

Why those coins were unfit for the redemption of the tithe while the other Bar Kokhba coins were fit, I do not know.

4. According to the talmudic sources, Bar Kokhba only ruled for two and a half years. That is not enough time to build a Temple.

The Talmud relates that the Judean tyrant, Herod the Great, rebuilt the Second Temple a few years before the common era.[9] Josephus Flavius, in his Antiquities of the Jews, states that Herod completely rebuilt the entire Temple compound, brick by brick. The task took only one and a half years.

21

The Bar Kokhba Dynasty

One of the great mysteries surrounding the Bar Kokhba epoch is the paucity of historical records, both religious and secular. An acknowledged Messiah seeking to overthrow the mighty Roman Empire should rate highly in the drama of the ancient world's political events. The greatest Roman general summoned from Britain to wage battle against the newly risen king of the Jews was certainly newsworthy. Why should there be a dark vacuum in the chronicles of the times? Historians seek to dispel the aura of mystery by explaining that the Bar Kokhba epoch lasted a mere two and a half years. The lone pretender to the throne of Judea was a small ripple in the mighty ocean of Roman events. It is no wonder that those events were not deemed noteworthy.

However, there are two rabbinical sources that claim that the Bar Kokhba revolt spanned more than two decades and there were three messianic kings comprising a Bar Kokhba Dynasty. If these sources are correct, the mystery only deepens.

Rabbi Menachem Meiri, a thirteenth-century rabbinic scholar, is considered among the giants is the realm of talmudic interpretation and exegesis. His encyclopedia of rabbinical thought and commentary is considered a classic and is still widely used. In his introduction to Avos, Meiri writes the following:

> During [the second and third] generation [of mishnaic teachers] Ben Koziba rose up and proclaimed himself the messiah. Many mistakenly followed after him, even Rebbe Akiva, who became his greatest supporter. Bar Kokhba revolted against the Roman emperor Domitian [?], and killed the governor [of Judea]. [Bar Kokhba] reigned in Betar, 52 years after the destruction of the Temple [122 C.E.]. After the death [of Bar Kokhba], he was succeeded by his son and eventually his grandson. [The dynasty lasted] until the emperor Hadrian ascended [the throne of Rome], 73 years after the destruction [of the Temple, in 143 C.E.], and killed the grandson of Ben Koziba.[1]

Meiri states that the Bar Kokhba revolution began under the Roman Emperor Domitian, 81 C.E.–96 C.E. In our texts of Meiri, the name Domitian is in brackets. Domitian assumed the Roman throne eleven years after the destruction of the Temple. Meiri says that the revolt began fifty-two years after the destruction, or 122 C.E., twenty-six years after Domitian died. Obviously, the name Domitian is an error. But what is the correct name?

Meiri also says that Hadrian killed Bar Kokhba's grandson in 143 C.E. Hadrian had died in 138 C.E. It is assumed by historians that Hadrian suppressed the Bar Kokhba revolution some time around 135 C.E. Meiri's date seems to be off by about eight years (143–135 = 8). If we subtract eight years from the dates given by Meiri, we find that the Bar Kokhba revolution began about forty-four years after the destruction of the Temple, in 114 C.E., and the revolt ended about sixty-five years after the destruction, in 135 C.E.

Trajan was the emperor in 114 C.E. That was the time of the Second Revolt in Judea against Rome. Hadrian was emperor in

135 c.e. That was the time of the Third Revolt and the death of Bar Kokhba in Betar.

In summary, the Bar Kokhba Dynasty started during the Second Revolt, under Trajan, circa 114 c.e., and ended twenty-one years later, after the Third Revolt and under Hadrian, circa 135 c.e. (In the next chapter we shall try to arrive at a more accurate date for the beginning of the Bar Kokhba revolution and try to account for the error that crept into Meiri.)

These facts can be confirmed from another rabbinical source, which follows along the lines of the Meiri but contains many more details. The quote is from *Seder HaDoros:*

Ben Koziba, called Bar Kokhba, who Rebbe Akiva proclaimed to be the [messianic] Star of Jacob, rebelled against the Romans. He wrought a great massacre against the Romans and the Greeks in Africa, like the sands of the seas, without number, and likewise in Egypt.

Also the [Jewish] inhabitants of Alexandria killed more than 200,000 Romans. Likewise, the Jews of Cyprus killed the gentiles until none were left.

He proclaimed himself to be the Messiah and Rebbe Akiva said that he was the messianic king.

. . . 52 years after the destruction [of the Temple, 122 c.e.], Bar Kokhba rose up. Because he rebelled against the [earlier] emperor, Trajan, he was called [by the Romans] Bar Koziba, son of deceit.

As mentioned before, he proclaimed himself the Messiah and the dynasty ruled Israel three generations. Romulus, the son of Rufus, the son of Ben Koziba.

Hadrian the emperor came against Romulus on the Ninth of Av in Betar, 52 years after the destruction of the Temple – some say 73 years, which was the year 3901 [143 c.e.]. A great massacre occurred among the Jews [of Betar]. Rebbe Akiva and his colleagues were among them. The city was so devastated that its location is no longer known.

. . . the Kosibean dynasty lasted 21 years, . . . Romulus ruled in Betar 2½ years.[2]

Both Meiri and the *Seder HaDoros* state there was a Bar Kokhba Dynasty, which lasted for three generations. The *Seder HaDoros* gives us the names of the three kings: Ben Koziba, Rufus the son of Ben Koziba, and Romulus the grandson of Ben Koziba. Though the names *Rufus* and *Romulus* are somewhat suspect, they are noteworthy. (Rufus is a Roman name meaning "red-head" or "ruddy." It was a Romanization of the Hebrew name *Reuben* or *Reuvain*.)

Both Meiri and the *Seder HaDoros* state that the dynasty began during the Second Revolt, during the reign of Trajan, circa 114 C.E., and ended twenty-one years later in Betar, during the reign of Hadrian.

It is also interesting to note that the *Seder HaDoros* attributes the name Bar Koziba, Son of Deceit, to the Romans. The Jerusalem Talmud attributes it to Rabbi Yochanan Tortah.[3]

If these sources are correct that Bar Kokhba founded a dynasty that lasted for twenty-one years, the impact of the revolution was greater than has yet been suspected.

22

Dating the Revolution

F rom the preceding chapter we discovered that Shimon Bar Kokhba began his uprising during the reign of Trajan, circa 114 C.E. Historians call this rebellion the Second Revolt, but they do not attribute it to the leadership of Bar Kokhba.

Over the course of the past quarter century, several ancient letters and documents that were written during the Bar Kokhba Era have come to light. One of these documents, referred to as Murrabba'at # 24, reads as follows:

On the 20th of Shevat
Year Two of the freedom of Israel
Shimon Ben Kosiba, Prince of Israel
In the camp at Herodium
I, Yehuda Ben Rabbah, said to Hillel Ben Garis that of my free will I have rented from you today land . . . which you have leased from Shimon Ben Kosiba, Prince of Israel.
This land I have rented from you from today until the end of the eve of the Sabbatical year, which is five complete years of harvest.

The document states that the land was to be rented for a period of five complete harvests, which would terminate at the end of the eve of the sabbatical year. A sabbatical year consists of a seven-year cycle. That means that the document was drawn up during the second year of the cycle. The opening date of the document stated that it was the second year of the Bar Kokhba rebellion. That means the the second year of the rebellion was the second year of the sabbatical cycle. The rebellion must have begun during the first year of the sabbatical cycle.

The Talmud states that the year when the Temple was destroyed was the first year of the sabbatical cycle.[1] The commonly accepted date for the year of the destruction is the year 70 C.E. Hebrew years and sabbatical cycles begin and end in the month of Tishrei (September/October). That means the year beginning September/October 69 and ending September/October 70 was the first year of the cycle.

The next sabbatical cycle began in 76/77 C.E., the following cycle began in 83/84, subsequent cycles began in 90/91, 97/98, 104/105, 111/112, 118/119, 125/126, and 132/133.

Trajan ruled from 99 C.E. until 117 C.E. There were only two first years of a sabbatical cycle during his reign, 104/105 and 111/112. By all accounts, the Second Revolt occurred during the later part of Trajan's rule. That would make the year 111/112 the most likely choice for the beginning of the Bar Kokhba revolution.

The document is telling us that the rebellion of 111/112 began forty-two years after destruction of the Temple. According to Meiri and the *Seder HaDoros*, it lasted twenty-one years, until 132/133.

Both Meiri and the *Seder HaDoros* state that the rebellion began fifty-two years after the destruction and ended seventy-three years after it. We have seen that the seventy-three-year figure cannot be correct since seventy-three years after the destruction is the year 143 C.E. and Hadrian died in 138 C.E. They both indicated that the rebellion started 52 years after the destruction, in 122 c.e., under the rule of Trajan, yet Trajan had died in 117 c.e. What accounts for the errors of Meiri and the *Seder HaDoros?*

The figure of fifty-two years comes from the Jerusalem Talmud. It states: "Fifty-two years after the destruction was the incident of Betar."[2]

Based on that quote, Meiri and *Seder HaDoros* assumed the revolt began fifty-two years after the destruction. From some as-yet unexplained source they knew that the Bar Kokhba dynasty lasted for twenty-one years. They therefore assumed that the revolt ended in 143 c.e. However, the revolt actually began in 111/112, as seen from the Bar Kokhba letter quoted previously. It was the later seige of Betar that began in 122 c.e., fifty-two years after the destruction of the Temple.

The revolt of 111/112 c.e. was led by the first of the Bar Kokhba dynasty, Shimon. Though his first name is not recorded in any of the talmudic or rabbinic literature, the name is known from coins, letters, and documents of that era. I believe, and *Doros HaRishonim* concurs, that during this period Jerusalem was recaptured.[3] Rebbe Akiva proclaimed him to be the Messiah. Shimon reigned in Jerusalem for only two and a half years, and then he died. I say that he ruled only for two and a half years because of a quote in the Talmud: "Bar Kokhba ruled 2½ years."[4]

One may argue that perhaps the Talmud refers to a two and a half year rule in Betar. That cannot be. The rule in Betar began in 122 c.e., according to the Jerusalem Talmud. It ended in 132/133 c.e. The Roman siege of Betar began 128/129 c.e. This is based on another statement in the Jerusalem Talmud that says that the siege of Betar lasted for three and a half years.[5]

The seat of the Bar Kokhba Dynasty was moved from Jerusalem to Betar because the Romans recaptured the Holy City, probably under Trajan. How long had the Jews been in possession of Jerusalem? The Talmud states that the Hasmonean

Dynasty lasted seventy years, the Herodian Dynasty lasted fifty years, and Bar Kokhba ruled for two and a half years.[6]

Rashi posed the question that although it is known from Seder Olam that both the Hasmonean and Herodian dynasties lasted 103 years each, the Talmud says that they lasted for 70 years and 50 years, respectively. Rashi resolves the problem by explaining that the Talmud is only reckoning the years for which the dynasties survived in honor and glory. Though the Hasmonean Dynasty lasted 103 years, only 70 years were years of glory. Though the Herodian Dynasty also lasted 103 years, only 50 of those years were years of glory.

If the Talmud is only considering years of glory, then the final years of the Bar Kokhba Dynasty cannot be considered years of glory. Jerusalem was under the dominion of Rome. The rebels were confined to Betar. The only years of glory that dynasty enjoyed were the years in Jerusalem.

The Talmud is stating that the years of glory for Bar Kokhba were two and a half years. Therefore, the Jews only had possession of the Holy City for two and a half years.

According to our calculations, the revolt ended circa 132 C.E. It is of interest to note that during the Bar Kokhba rebellion, the Jews restruck Roman coins. The latest known Roman coin to be restruck was from the year 132. It may also be of interest to note that, as explained earlier, Shimon Bar Kokhba had died under the rule of Trajan. *Doros HaRishonim* mentions that all known Bar Kokhba coins that have the name Shimon on them are all restruck Trajan coins.[7] No restruck Hadrianic coins have the name Shimon on them.

23

The Abba Inscription

During the early 1970s, while construction work was being done in the Givat HaMivtar section of Jerusalem, north of the Old City, burial caves were discovered. The remains of thirty-five Jews were found. One male was the victim of crucifixion, two died from fire, one suffered from a fatal arrow wound, one was clubbed to death, and three children died of starvation. The others seemed to have died of natural causes.

The burial practice in ancient Jerusalem was to inter the body, without a coffin, in the earth. After a year's time, when the body had decomposed and only the skeleton remained, the bones were transferred to a stone coffin, called an ossuary.

The wealthier aristocrats had large, ornate ossuaries, which very often contained an inscription. This ossuary would contain only the bones of one individual or, occasionally, the remains of a husband and wife. The poorer citizenry would have the remains of an entire family stored in a single, small ossuary. The ossuaries were placed in the walls of man-made burial caves.

One inscription found on a Givat HaMivtar ossuary reads as follows: "I, Abba son of the priest Elazer, son of Aaron the High

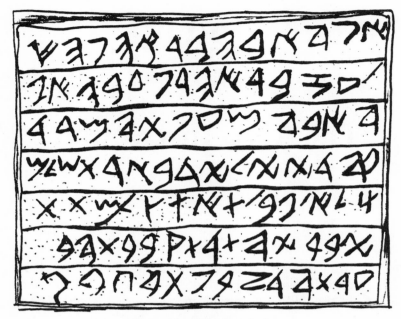

Plate 14 The Abba Inscription.

[Priest], I, Abba, the oppressed and persecuted, who was born in Jerusalem and exiled to Babylonia, brought [back to Jerusalem the remains of] Matisyahu bar Yehuda and I buried him in this cave, which I acquired by document" (see Plate 14).

There are several unusual characteristics of this inscription. First, it details the identity of the one doing the burial more than the one being buried. This would seem to indicate that the one who brought back the remains of Matisyahu was a man of renown, more so than the deceased.

Second, since Abba was a priest, why was it necessary for him to say that he was also a descendant of Aaron the High Priest? All priests were descendants of Aaron.

Third, the script is in Paleo-Hebrew, an ancient form of lettering that was preeminent during the First Temple Era. Yet

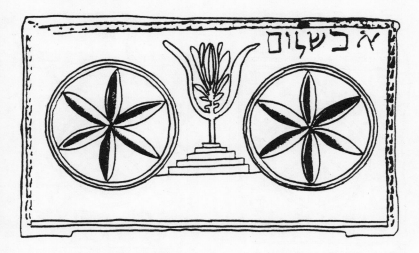

Plate 15 Rossette decorations on ossuary.

the ornamentation of the neighboring ossuaries and pottery fragments indicate a late–Second Temple, or even post–Second Temple, style. Why would a single ancient ossuary be found with remains interred five hundred years later?

Fourth, who persecuted Abba and why was he driven out of Jerusalem?

Fifth, several of the ossuaries found at the site display a design consisting of a six-pointed star rosette surrounded by two concentric circles (see Plate 15). Was this some sort of popular design or did it represent something?

Before Bar Kokhba invaded and captured Jerusalem from the Roman garrison that was stationed there, he lived in the Judean Desert. Bar Kokhba and his revolutionaries constructed many hundreds of underground towns, not unlike the burrows of prairie dogs. Over three hundred of them have been discovered in the past thirty years. Many revolutionary groups also lived in the caves that dot the desert mountains.

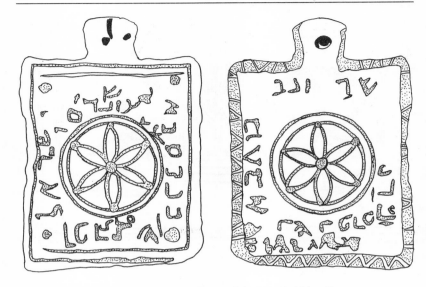

Plate 16a & 16b The two faces of the Bar Kokhba plaque.

In the winter of 1987, a group of archaeologists discovered a small metal plaque in one of the underground towns. The plaque was approximately 3½ inches by 3 inches and had been used as a weight in ancient times. On both the front and back of the weight was the design of a six-pointed star rosette surrounded by two concentric circles. Around the outer circle was writing. The inscription read: "Shimon Ben Kosiba, Prince of Israel" (see Plates 16a and 16b).

Could it be that the star design represented the "Star of Jacob," Bar Kokhba, which was Rebbe Akiva's name for Ben Kosiba? On some of the Bar Kokhba coins is a star, symbolizing the Star of Jacob. We know from Bar Kokhba letters found in the desert caves that Bar Kokhba also reinstituted the use of Paleo-Hebrew script in an attempt to revitalize the nationalistic spirit.

This suggests that the tomb discovered in Givat HaMivtar was a burial site used during the Bar Kokhba rebellion. That would explain the star design on the ossuaries and the Paleo-Hebrew script. But who was this Abba, the one who buried the body?

When Bar Kokhba ruled in Jerusalem, he appointed a High Priest, Elazer. His name appears on some of the Bar Kokhba coins. Possibly, this Abba was the son of Elazer the High Priest. That would explain why Abba called himself "Abba son of Elazer the Priest, son of Aaron the High Priest."

In all probability, Abba, who had been born in Jerusalem, was driven out during the Trajan persecution. When Bar Kokhba recaptured the Holy City, Abba was able to return, bringing back the body of Matisyahu bar Yehuda with him.

The so-called Abba Inscription, which heretofore has been rendered as unfathomable, in light of the above, should now be reclassified as a priceless historical document.

24

From Givat Hamivtar, Jerusalem, to Bat Creek, Tennessee

In 1889, the Smithsonian Institute in Washington, D.C., sponsored an archaeological dig along the banks of the Little Tennessee River to excavate Indian burial mounds. Near the mouth of Bat Creek, three mounds were discovered. The smallest was twenty-eight feet across and five feet high. At the bottom of this mound, nine skeletons were found. They were arranged in two rows. The first row contained two skeletons. The second row had seven. All of the skeletons were placed with the heads pointing north, except one: one skeleton in the row of 7 lay with it head pointing to the south. Under the skull of those remains, a small plaque was found (Plate 17).

The stone plaque measures 4½ inches in length and 1¾ inches in width. Nine letters or characters are inscribed on the plaque. The ninth letter is mostly obscured due to a crack in the stone. The director of the project, Cyrus Thomas, "identified" the letters as being Cherokee writing. Thomas based his conclusion solely on the fact that the plaque was found in Cherokee Territory. The plaque was photographed, and the photo was duly added to an album of Indian curiosities and filed away. The stone was stored away in some backroom of the

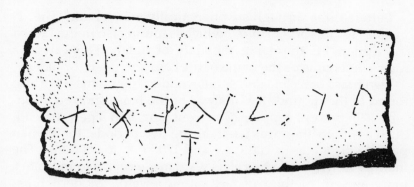

Plate 17 The Bat Creek Inscription.

National Museum of Natural History. Both the photograph and the stone were forgotten.

Both were forgotten possibly because the photograph was printed upside down. In the middle 1950s and early 1970s, several scholars noticed the strong resemblance of these letters to Paleo-Hebrew characters. Finally, almost a century after its discovery, Professor Cyrus Gordon, a Semitic languages scholar, identified the letters as Paleo-Hebrew and very similar to the letters of the "Abba Inscription." The first two letters and the last two letters of the nine-letter inscription were not positively identifiable.

Below is a listing of the letters:

1. zayin[?], raish[?]
2. kuf[?]
3. lamed
4. yud
5. heh
6. vov
7. daleth
8. mem[?]
9. aleph[?], vav[?], somech[?]

Letters three through six phonetically are "lyhud." The "l" means "to" or "of." "Yhud," which is found also in the "Abba Inscription," is the name Yehudah, or Judah. This can be a man's first name or the name of the country Judah, or Judea. Two brass bracelets and some wooden fragments were also found in the mound. An analysis of the brass showed a content of 70 percent copper, 27 percent zinc, and 3 percent lead. Such a composition was used during two periods: the Roman period, 100 B.C.E. to 200 C.E., and 1700 C.E. to 1900 C.E. The manner in which the bracelets were made seems to indicate a more ancient method of fashioning jewelry. Modern brass bracelets were cast in the shape of a straight thick wire and then bent in the shape of the letter "C." The more ancient method was to cast a strip of brass, fold it over to give it a round shape, and then bend it to form the letter "C." The folding method would give the bracelet a hollow core. The two bracelets found in the Bat Creek Mound had hollow cores.

The wood fragments were radiocarbon dated to show the wood was cut from the tree somewhere between 32 C.E. and 769 C.E.

What does this inscription mean historically and archaeologically? It does not mean much, I'm afraid. Although it grips the imagination to realize that ancient Judean artifacts from the Bar Kokhba Era have found their way to the shores of the New World, it is impossible to assess its meaning. Does it prove that Jews inhabited the backwoods of Tennessee thirteen hundred years before Columbus? (Why would they choose such a remote area to inhabit?) Does it merely indicate that some ancient Indians buried some Judean artifacts bartered or captured from a voyager in Bat Creek? Or is this some elaborate hoax?

To be sure, there are those who suspect that the "finds" were planted there by John W. Emmert, assistant to the Smithsonian's Cyrus Thomas. Frank Moore Cross, a former professor of Oriental languages at Harvard, rendered the script indecipherable.

The debate over the Jews of Bat Creek, Tennessee, continues in academic circles. Personally, I feel that more information is needed before serious attention is to be given the finds. But it is too late to do further excavations in the area. The Tennessee Valley Authority project built a dam, which flooded the mouth of Bat Creek. The burial mound now lies under the newly created Lake Tellico.

So much for Indian burial mounds of Bat Creek, Tennessee — we now head back to the burial caves of Givat HaMivtar, Jerusalem.

25

Simon—The Temple Builder

Another one of the ossuaries found in the Givat HaMivtar burial vault contains an amazing inscription. This ossuary, which now rests in the Israel Museum in Jerusalem among other period ossuaries, reads simply: "Simon, Builder of the Temple" (see Plate 18). This intriguing inscription remains a mystery.

Earlier, I suggested that Bar Kokhba built a Messianic Temple on Mount Moriah. Could it be that this is the ossuary of Bar Kokhba's Temple builder, the overseer of the holy task, who was a man named Simon?

Another thought occurred to me. The Hebrew first name of Bar Kokhba was Shimon. This is known from the many Bar Kokhba letters discovered in the Judean desert and from the Bar Kokhba coins minted in Jerusalem, which contained his full name, Shimon Bar Kokhba. The ossuary has the name, Simon. The phrase, "Builder of the Temple" is written in Aramaic, "banah heichalah." Simon is the Aramaic name for Shimon. Could it be . . .

The ossuary contained the remains of two individuals, one male and one female. Both died of natural causes. The male

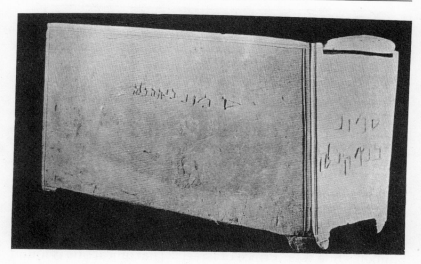

Plate 18 Ossuary bearing the inscription "Simon the Builder of the Temple."

was 5 feet 8 inches tall, very robust, and powerfully built. His age at death was approximately forty-seven. The female, presumably his wife, was 5 feet 6 inches tall and died around the age of thirty.

Is it possible that this ossuary contains the very remains of Shimon Bar Kokhba, the one who built the Temple, the one who Rebbe Akiva proclaimed to be the King—the Messiah? But wasn't Bar Kokhba executed in Betar? This rugged individual was buried in Jerusalem and died of natural causes.

Meiri and the *Seder HaDoros* stated that there were three kings in the Bar Kokhba Dynasty. The third, Romulus, was the one who was executed in Betar. The first, Shimon, could very well have died of natural causes in Jerusalem.

The Jerusalem Talmud says that the Messiah was born the same day the Second Temple was destroyed, or 70 C.E.[1] Simon died at approximately age forty-seven. If Simon is Shimon Bar Kokhba, that means that he died circa 117 C.E. The second

Plate 19 The "Nazirite" Ossuary.

member of the royal dynasty, Rufus, was then appointed the successor to the throne. This is wholly consistent with the historical sequence of events.

As much as I'd like to believe that these are the remains of the legendary Shimon Bar Kokhba, it is quite doubtful. Shimon's title was "Prince of Israel." That offical title is found on coins and weights of the period and it is missing from the ossuary. The ossuary is also lacking the ornate detail one would expect for the final resting place of the founder of the Messianic Dynasty.

Not far from the Givat Hamivtar burial site, another tomb was discovered. This tomb, which is located on Mount Scopus, contained ten ossuaries. One of the ossuaries is beautifully ornamented with a floral and grape design. Based on the inscriptions found there, it was the burial place of the family of Jonathan the Nazir, or Nazirite (see Plate 19). Although archaeologists assume that this Jonathan was a nazirite—one who made an oath to abstain from grapes, from cutting his hair, and coming in contact with a corpse—the term *nazir* also refers to a person with a claim to royalty. Purple is the color of royalty. Ripe grape clusters are also purple. It is no wonder that grape vines laden with luscious clusters of grapes was the symbol chosen to represent royalty.

Jacob's son, Joseph, was called "the nazir of his brothers."[2] Siforno and Rashbam say that the word *nazir* is related to *nezer*, or crown.[3] A nazir is a person with a claim to the throne. This Jonathan was a royal nazir, or more simply put, a prince, and so he rated a beautifully ornamented ossuary. Had Simon the Temple Builder been the same as Shimon Bar Kokhba, he, too, would have merited a finely decorated ossuary.

There is the possibility that Shimon died shortly before the Romans retook the Holy City and thus there was no time to prepare an ornate ossuary as befitted a man of Shimon's messianic stature. The customary title of "Prince of Israel" may have been omitted by the stone carver because the futility of the struggle was quickly becoming apparent.

As with much of this enigmatic era, we can only speculate and wonder.

26

Remains of Aelia Capitolina

To celebrate the destruction of the Second Temple and the downfall of Judea, the conquerors had built an arch of triumph in the Roman Forum. To celebrate the collapse of the Bar Kokhba revolt, Hadrian also built his own arch of triumph, the conquered capital of Judea itself, Jerusalem. Jerusalem was converted into a Roman garrison and renamed Aelia Capitolina (see Plate 20). The Temple Mount, which was the most sacred site to the Jews, was now brazenly defiled with a pagan temple to honor Jupiter.

The area of Hadrian's Aelia Capitolina was the very same as is now occupied by the walled Old City of Jerusalem. The Jerusalem of Temple times had been a much larger city. The old walls had been destroyed and Hadrian did not have any grandiose plans for the former Jewish capital. New walls were built, but encompassing a smaller area. Over the course of centuries, Aelia Capitolina's walls were torn down and newer walls were built. Part of the Aelia Capitolina wall can still be seen along the southern wall of the Old City, near the present-day Dung Gate.

The main entrance into Aelia Capitolina was through its northern gate. A triple archway was built into the wall, with a dedication plaque reading: *COL AEL CAP D D* (*the Coloney of*

Plate 20 Map of Aelia Capitolina.

Aelia Capitolina by order of the Council). Inside the gateway was a large, semicircular plaza. In the center of the plaza was a single, large column with a statue of Hadrian on top.

The remains of the triple gateway and the plaque are still visible today, below the Damascus Gate (see Plate 21). A nineteenth-century plaza inside the gateway, called the Column Plaza, marks the spot where the marble column with Hadrian's statue once stood. This is the gateway to the present-day Moslem Quarter.

At the southern end of the Aelia Capitolina plaza were two streets. One street went southeast through the city, following the valley called Tyropean. Called Cardo Valencia, it passed along the western Temple Mount wall and led to the southern gate, which is today called the Dung Gate.

The other street went southwest, across Mount Zion, and led to the other southern gate, which is today called the Zion Gate. This street was called Cardo Maximus.

Plate 21 Partial view of the remains of the triple gateway.

The main east-west street started at the eastern gate of the city, which is today called the Jaffa Gate. It was called Decumanus. It led eastward, crossing Cardo Maximus, and terminated where it met Cardo Valencia, opposite the middle of the western Temple wall. At the intersection of Decumanus and Cardo Maximus there was a tetrapylon. A tetrapylon consisted of four large columns, set apart and forming a square, supporting arches that went from capital to capital. Remains of these capitals are still there, inside an old Turkish cafe.

These three main streets of Aelia Capitolina were patterned after three streets that had preexisted in Temple times. The Romans had the streets repaved and lined the sides of the 40-foot-wide thoroughfares with colonades consisting of a series of 16-foot-high columns supporting a wooden roof. Under the colonades were stores.

For two thousand years, these three streets served as the main arteries of Jerusalem as well as the business districts. Part of the Cardo Maximus has been uncovered in recent years, and where ancient stores sold the necessities of life, today modern stores cater to the tourist, selling upscale women's apparel and expensive silver items. Some of the original street, columns, and stores have been uncovered.

The course of the Decumanus is still there and serves as the site of the Arab shuq, where Arab vendors continue to hawk everything from Persian melons to olive-wood camels and menorahs.

Aelia Capitolina had another street, called Via Dolorosa, that went east from Cardo Valencia out to the eastern gate of the city, today called the Lion's Gate. There was a triple arch spanning the street. The central arch was 17 feet wide and 20½ feet high. Parts of the arch are still there.

One of the most fascinating relics of Aelia Capitolina can be found on the southern Temple wall. There is a dedication plaque (see also Plate 22) that reads:

TITO AEL HADRIANO
ANTONINO AUG PIO
PP PONTIF AUGUR
DD

(To Titus Aelius Hadrianus
Antoninus Augustus Pius
of the Fatherland, Chief of the Diviners
by Order of the Council)

Where this plaque was originally located is not known. Some think it was the dedication stone of the Temple to Jupiter. When the temple was torn down by the fourth-century Christian Byzantines, the plaque was discarded. It was later found by the Moslems who used it to repair the southern Temple

Plate 22 Dedication Plaque, located in upper center.

wall. The stone was set in place, upside down, where it remains today.

Numerous bricks and tiles with the letters LXF, the identification of the Roman Tenth Legion, were found to the south and southwest of the Temple Mount, indicating that many Roman houses were built in that area. Some of the bricks bearing the letters AE C C (Aelia Colonia Capitolinia) were also found there.

Eusebius, in his *Ecclesiastical History,* writes that Hadrian decreed, "The Jewish nation should be absolutely prevented from entering thenceforth even the district around Jerusalem so that not even from a distance it could be seen."[1] Justin Martyr, in his *Apology,* says that violators of the decree were subject to the death penalty.[2] Tertullian, in *Answer to the Jews,* says the decree included the city of Bethlehem.[3]

Foreign nations sought to destroy the Jewish People, not only physically and spiritually, but also emotionally, by obliterating the sacred monuments of their glorious past and denying the mourning Jews even the sight of the land where their monuments once stood. They tried to eradicate the memory of Jerusalem as though it had never existed. How ironic that today it is the Jews who seek to restore and preserve the monuments of those same nations, nations which no longer exist.

III

THE JEWISH DOCTRINE
OF THE MESSIAH

27

The Messiah in Light of History

The Bar Kokhba epoch presents a unique opportunity in the realm of religious doctrine. Rebbe Akiva proclaimed Bar Kokhba to be the messianic king. Many theological discussions concerning the future Messiah took place after the Bar Kokhba Era. It should be of some intellectual and religious interest to examine those discussions in light of the events that had already taken place.

The practice of approaching religious dogma through the hindsight offered by history originates with Maimonides. The question was raised whether the Messiah will be called upon to work miracles as a sign of his authenticity. Maimonides suggested that no such demands will be made of the Messiah. He offers proof from the fact that Rebbe Akiva did not require Bar Kokhba to prove his claim by performing miracles. From Maimonides' precedent, we can establish the veracity of interpreting religious philosophy in terms of historical events.

There is a rather large body of prophetic, talmudic, and midrashic thought on the subject of the Messiah and the End of Days. This body of work can be divided into two distinct parts. One part is written in a fanciful, kabbalist style and language. The ideas expressed are not to be taken literally but rather represent concepts known only to those initiated in the aggadic traditions of the Sages. The second part is a dogmatic analysis by the rabbinical scholars concerning the doctrine of the Messiah. On occasion, it is difficult to determine into which division a particular prophetic vision or talmudic discussion falls. However, it is those tenets that can be determined to be taken literally that will concern us at present.

The various issues and questions that will be discussed in the subsequent chapters are:

1. What physical and spiritual attributes are ascribed to the Messiah?

2. Are these attributes ascribed only to one individual or are there many potential Messiahs who possess these qualities?

3. When will the Messiah come?

4. The Sages mention a Messiah, son of David, and a Messiah, son of Joseph. What are their respective roles?

5. The Messianic Era will herald the war of Gog and Magog. Who are Gog and Magog?

6. What role will the Prophet Elijah play in the Messianic Era?

7. How will the Messianic Era differ from present-day life?

8. How does the Resurrection of the Dead relate to the Messianic Era?

9. Will the Third Temple be built before the advent of the Messiah?

10. Was Rebbe Akiva wrong in proclaiming Bar Kokhba to be the Messiah?

28

Messiah the Man

The prophet Isaiah proclaimed, *"There shall come a rod from the stem of Jesse [the father of David]. . . . And the spirit of the Lord shall rest upon him, the spirit of wisdom and understanding, the spirit of counsel and might, the spirit of knowledge and of the fear of the Lord"*[1] (emphasis mine).

Isaiah describes the Messiah as a man of great spiritual character. He does not describe him physically or reveal his family background, other than the fact that he is a descendant of King David's family. This lack of physical description can be understood in light of Rabbi Ovadiah Bartenurah's contention that the Messiah is not one specific, predetermined individual, but rather each generation has a unique person who possesses the spiritual attributes that would qualify him as the Messiah, should the world merit his coming.[2]

The Talmud records:

The school of Rabbi Shila said that the Messiah's name is Shiloh, as it written "until Shiloh [the pacifier, the Messiah] comes" (Genesis 49:10). The school of Rabbi Yannai said that the Messiah's name is Yinnon, as it is written "[Messiah's]

name is Yinnon [the ruler]" (Psalm 72:17). The school of Rabbi
Chaniniah said that the Messiah's name is Chaniniah [he who
offers favor], as it is written "I will give unto you Chananiah"
(Jeremiah 16:13).[3]

The students in each academy felt that their rabbi had the
great spiritual qualities of the Messiah. Since the Messiah
could come at any time, there has to be at least one individual
who possesses the moral and intellectual attributes and could
qualify to be the Messiah.

Concerning the name or title of the Messiah, Abarbanel (Maiy-
onai Hayeshua) writes that the commonly given title to the future
redeemer of mankind is Messiah. However, the term *Messiah*, or
Moshiach in Hebrew, merely means the "anointed" or "the designated." The word can refer to any great person who was divinely
designated for a sacred purpose. It does not refer specially to the
Messiah. However, common usage has consigned the word to
refer specially to the Messianic redeemer.

Where is the identity of the Messiah supposed to be revealed? Maimonides (Igeres Yemen) wrote in his famous "Letter to Yemen" that the revelation will occur in the land of Israel.
Yalkut Shemoni indicates that it will take place in Jerusalem on
the Temple Mount.[4]

Midrash Tanchumah says that the Messiah will be greater
than Moses our teacher.[5] This presents two difficulties. First,
how could the students of the various academies believe that
their teacher had spiritual qualities equal to the Messiah's if
the Messiah's qualities surpassed those of Moses? Surely they
did not think that their masters were greater than Moses.
Second, the Torah itself testifies that "there will never arise
again in Israel a prophet like Moses."[6]

Rabbi Yonnasan Eibschutz explains that the extent of rule
and the authority of the Messiah will surpass that of Moses.[7]
However, no one will ever arise who can even approach the
prophetic ability of Moses.

Maimonides writes that the wisdom of the Messiah will surpass that of the renowned King Solomon.[8] Utilizing his holy spirit, the Messiah will determine the tribal ancestry of the Jewish People.[9]

The prophet Isaiah continues, *"And he shall judge not according to the sight of his eyes nor decide according to the hearing of his ears but with righteousness shall he judge the poor and decide fairly for the meek of the earth"*[10] (emphasis mine).

The Talmud explains Isaiah's prophecy to the effect that the Messiah will not have to rely on his eyes and ears but rather will be able to smell the odor of truth.[11] This test was put to Bar Kokhba, who failed the test and was killed.

Maimonides also writes that the Messiah will not be required to offer signs or work miracles to justify his messianic claim.[12] Yet the Talmud says that Bar Kokhba was tested to see if he could smell truth, which certainly would seem to indicate that the rabbis were looking for some supernatural sign or miracle.

I believe that the Talmud's phrase of "smelling the truth" is not to be taken in the literal sense that truth has an odor. Rather, it means that every person has a spiritual quality or aura about him or her. This spiritual emanation can be either good or evil. The Messiah, being a person of great spiritual qualities, will be sensitive to these emanations. He will not have to rely only on visible evidence and audible testimony, but will utilize his sensitivities in rendering justice. Our Sages do not regard this sensitivity as a wonder or miracle. In fact, the Talmud states that one is not allowed to render a judicial decision based on miracles or supernatural events.[13] A spiritual sensitivity to truth and justice is not a metaphysical phenomena but rather a natural occurrence in the realm of righteousness and holiness.

29

When Will the Messiah Come?

"When will the Messiah come?" asked Rebbe Yehoshua ben Levi. "Today," answered the future redeemer, "today, if you harken to [God's] voice."[1]

Our Sages have long pondered the great mystery regarding the time of the Messiah's expected arrival. His appearance would mark the end the Roman exile and herald the new Messianic Age. The Egyptian exile was foretold to last four hundred years. The Babylonian exile was foretold to last seventy years. Our Sages had hoped that there would be some hint in the words of the Prophets as to the duration of the Roman exile that began on the day the Holy Temple was destroyed.

Searching through the words of the prophets, various Sages came to different conclusions. Some Sages thought the Diaspora would last 1,400 years. They based their prediction on the verse in Daniel (7:25), *"a time and times and half the time"* (emphasis mine). The term "time" referred to the length of the exile in Egypt, which lasted 400 years. "Time" equaled 400 years. "Times" meant twice 400 years, or 800 years, and "half the time" meant 200 years, totaling 1,400 years. The Messiah would appear 1,400 years after the destruction of the Second Temple. That would be the year 1470 C.E.[2]

Rebbe Simlai thought the Diaspora would last 1,410 years and the Messiah would appear in 1480 C.E. He based his prognostication on the verse in Psalms (80:6), "*give them tears to drink a third time*" (emphasis mine). The Diaspora would last three times as long as the combined Egyptian exile (400 years) and Babylonian exile (70 years).[3]

Rebbe Akiva taught that the Diaspora would be short-lived. He based his prediction on the verse in Haggai (2:6), "*it is a short while, and I will shake the heavens and earth*" (emphasis mine). It is no wonder that Rebbe Akiva was prepared to proclaim Bar Kokhba the Messiah only a few decades after the destruction of the Temple.

However, the other Sages maintained that Rebbe Akiva's verse does not reflect the Messianic Era, but rather the glory of the Hasmonean, Herodian, and Bar Kokhba eras.[4]

The Talmud even records a report of the Messiah's due arrival from a scroll found in the archives in Rome.

Rav Channan bar Tachlifa sent word to Rav Yosef: I found a certain man who had a scroll in his possession. It was written with Assyrian characters in the Hebrew language. I asked him how he came [by the scroll]. He told me that he was a Roman mercenary and he found it among the Roman archives. Written [in the scroll] was the following—4,231 [or 4,291] years after the creation, the world will become orphaned. [After which] will be the war of the monstrous sea creatures, [after which] will be the war of Gog and Magog. Then will be the Messianic Era. God will not renew His universe until after 7,000 years. Rav Acha son of Rabah said after 5,000 years.[5]

Some of the Sages tried to disuade others from contemplating the imponderable.

Rabbi Nathan says: This verse goes to the very depths of the matter, ". . . *for it is yet to come the vision for that appointed time*"

(Hab. 2:3) (emphasis mine). The End of Days has yet to be envisioned or predicted by the prophets.[6]

Whenever Rebbe Zeira found scholars engaged in calculating the arrival of the Messiah, he would beg them to stop. "Do not postpone his arrival," he would plead, "for the Messiah will only come unexpectedly."[7]

Rabbi Samuel bar Nachmani, realizing the danger of attempting to calculate the Messiah's arrival, said in the name of Rebbe Yonasson: "Blasted are the bones of those who predict the end, for should their prediction not be realized, people will abandon hope for him."[8]

There are three interpretations explaining the words of Rabbi Samuel bar Nachmani. Abarbanel explains that it is forbidden to divine the date of the Messiah's arrival through astrology.[9] However, it is permitted to calculate the End of Days through interpretation of the words of the prophets.

Ramban says that the prohibition to calculate the End of Days is only for those generations many years removed from the expected arrival.[10]

Maimonides says that is forbidden to conjecture the date of the Messianic Era under all circumstances.[11] Maimonides elaborates that the prophet Daniel predicted that many Sages would offer various theories as to when the Messiah would come. *"Many will run far and wide, opinions will increase"* (emphasis mine).[12]

If such predictions can lead to disaster, why were they made? Since there were conflicting dates, were some of the Sages wrong? Since all the predicted dates have passed, were all the Sages wrong?

Maimonides, in his "Letter to Yemen," answers these questions. The Sages did not approve of calculating and forecasting the arrival of the Messiah. However, in times of desperation, the Sages feared that many Jews would abandon the faith. In all sincerity, these Sages then sought to divine the arrival of the Messiah in order to give their fellow Jews the hope and strength to endure.

Were the conflicting dates incorrect? Maimonides points out that though the exile in Egypt was to last four hundred years and the exile to Babylonia was to be for seventy years, the exact time to begin the counting was unknown. Some thought that the four hundred years of Egyptian bondage began when Jacob came into Egypt. Some figured that it began when the Children of Israel were enslaved. Others calculated from the covenant of Abraham. When the Exodus finally occurred, it was realized that the four hundred years began the day Isaac was born.

Likewise, there were many opinions as to the exact beginning of the Babylonian exile. Did it begin when Nebuchadnezzar first invaded Jerusalem? Did it begin when King Joachim was captured? Not until the exile was over and the Jews returned to Israel did they realize that the seventy years began on the day their Temple was destroyed.

Traditionally, it has been understood that there was no "earliest" date on which the Messiah could arrive. Should the Jews merit his coming, he would arrive that very day. The date the Sages sought to divine was the latest possible date on which he would arrive should the Jews not merit his early arrival. This view is voiced in the following quotes from the Talmud.

Rebbe Yochanan said: The son of David will come either in a generation that is completely righteous or completely wicked.[13]

It was taught in the school of Elijah: The world will exist for six thousand years. [The first] two thousand years were empty [of Torah], [the middle] two thousand years [there was] Torah, and [the final] two thousand years will be the Messianic Era. Because of our sins, he did not come at the beginning of these final two thousand years.[14]

Rebbe Alexandri said: Rebbe Yehoshua ben Levi answered the following contradiction. It is written (Is. 60:22) "*I, the Lord,*

will hasten it [the redemption] in its time" (emphasis mine). "Hasten" implies that the Messiah will come early. "In its time"
implies he will not be early. If they are worthy, God will hasten
it; if not, he will come at the due time.[15]

Rebbe Alexandri said: Rebbe Yehoshua ben Levi answered
the following contradiction. One verse (Dan. 7:13) states *"Behold! One like the son of man came with the clouds of heaven."*
Another verse (Zech. 9:7) states *"lowly, riding upon an ass"*
(emphasis mine). If they are meritous, he will come "with the
clouds of heaven;" if they are not meritous, he will come
"lowly, riding upon an ass."[16]

Should the Jewish Nation not merit an early arrival of the
Messiah, he will come on the obscure, fixed date. The Sages
have painted a very dismal picture of that Premessianic Era.

Rabbi Yochanan said: "The generation in which the son of
David will come, scholars will be few, and the rest [of the
people], their eyes will fail from sorrow and grief. Great oppression and evil decrees will be renewed. Before one [trouble]
has ended a second will quickly come."[17]

Our Sages taught: The seven years before the coming of the
son of David, in the first year, the verse will be fulfilled *"I will
cause rain upon one city, and cause it not to rain upon the other"*
(Amos 4:7) (emphasis mine). In the second year, arrows of
hunger will be sent forth. In the third year, a great famine.
Men, women, children, and the righteous will perish. The
[schools of] Galilee will be in ruins. The [district of] Gablan will
lay desolate. The supreme court justices will wander from city
to city receiving no favor. The wisdom of the scribes will become repulsive; God-fearing men will be despised. The face of
the generation will be [shameless] like a mongrel cur. Truth will
become fractured.[18]

Rabbi Nehorai said: In the generation when the Messiah
comes, the young will humiliate the aged, the elders will stand
to honor the youth, daughters will rebel against their mothers,
and daughter-in-law against mother-in-law. The face of the

generation will be [shameless] like a mongrel cur. A son will not have shame before his father.[19]

Rabbi Nechemia said: In the generation when the Messiah comes, insolence will be great, respect will be perverted, the vine will yield its fruit [in abundance], yet [the cost of] wine will be exorbitant [because of the great demand]. The government will oppose religion. There will be none to rebuke.[20]

Our Rabbis taught: The son of David will not come until the informers are in abundance, scholars are few, the last coin [of hope] is gone from the purse, and all faith in the redemption is gone.[21]

Rebbe Yochanan said: When you see a generation overwhelmed by great difficulties like a river, hope for him [the Messiah]. As it is written (Is. 59:19), *"When the enemy comes like a flood, the spirit of the Lord shall raise the flag against him, and the redeemer shall come to Zion"* (emphasis mine).[22]

The Talmud calls the Premessianic Era, the "labor pains of the Messiah."[23] They envisioned that the Messiah would herald a new spiritual rebirth among the Jews and all the nations. Just as a human child is born amidst the pains of labor, so, too, the Jews will have to endure the tribulations of the birth of the Messianic Era. It is no wonder that the Talmud records Rebbe Yochanan, Rabah, and Ulah as saying, "Let him come, but let me not see him."[24]

Since tradition had foretold of a sorrowful era of persecution and oppression preceding the Messianic Era, it can readily be understood that the reigns of Trajan and Hadrian were deemed to be that very time at which the arrival of the Messiah seemed imminent.

30

Miraculous Manifestation or Political Process?

The Messianic Era of Bar Kokhba developed through military successes and political alliances. There was no miraculous parting of the seas or smiting with plagues. However, the redemption from Egypt did occur through Divine intervention. God Himself waged war on the enemies of the Jewish People and caused the dramatic deliverance. Should not that historic event establish precedence for the future deliverance of Israel? Why were miraculous spectacles and heavenly signs absent from the Bar Kokhba epoch?

Several of the commentaries correct our misimpression of the dawn of the future Messianic Era. Rabbi Moses ben Machir writes: "God's [future] salvation will come in the blink of the eye. This redemption will be easier than the redemption from Egypt, for this one could be through the natural sequence of events. There will be no need to disrupt the order of natural law, which was not the situation with the exodus from Egypt."[1]

Nachmanides confirms the concept of a natural political evolution into the Messianic Era.[2] Nachmanides writes, "With the consent of the nations and with their assistance will [the Jewish People again] enter the land of Israel [in the Messianic Era]."

Rabbi David Cordavaro lends historical support for the view that the Messiah will come through a natural process and sequence of events.[3] The Babylonian exile ended when the Persian emperor Cyrus granted the Jews permission to regain the Holy Land and rebuild their Temple. Supernatural phenomenon did not play any role in the ingathering of the Jews. So, too, in the Messianic Era, the Messiah will be hailed and acknowledged by the world leaders through the course of ordinary political occurrences.

The revered twentieth-century saint, Rabbi Israel Meir Kagan (known as Choffetz Chaim), reiterates these views.[4] He, too, mentions the ingathering of the Jews in the time of Cyrus.

However, there are significant sources that indicate the contrary, that the Messianic Era will come about through Divine intervention. The Midrash is replete with such indications:

In the days to come you shall be delivered by God, an everlasting deliverance.[5]

In this world you were saved by the hand of man. In Egypt [you were saved] through Moses and Aaron, in the days of Sisra through Barak and Deborah, etc. However, in the days to come, I alone will deliver you and you shall no longer be subjugated.[6]

Rebbe Berachia quoted Rebbe Chelbo who in turn quoted Rebbe Shmuel, "Neither Elijah nor the King Messiah will redeem Israel; God will redeem Israel."[7]

In the future God Himself will rebuild Jerusalem and gather in the exiled.[8]

One of the great Chassidic masters, Rabbi Moses Teiltelbaum (Yismach Moshe, Shimini), explained that all works and deeds wrought by man are subject to the ravages of time. Man's accomplishments can be undone. Since the Messianic Era will mark the climax of human history, when wars shall be abolished for everafter, it is difficult to imagine that such a state can be accomplished through Man. A state of permanent harmony and tranquility would seem to require a Divine decree.

We have before us contradictory statements concerning the Messianic Era. Some sources maintain that it will be a natural process, brought about by the political and military hands of Man. Other sources contend that the future era will be by divine decree. Rabbi Menachem Kasher, one of the twentieth century's most prolific rabbinic authors, resolves the conflict with an idea based on a concept conceived by Rabbi Don Yitzchok Abarbanel. Abarbanel explains that natural phenomena are predictable. They follow a set pattern determined by the laws of nature. However, rainfall, which we consider to be a natural phenomenon, is totally unpredictable. The amount of rain and the number of days of rain vary from year to year. Even in modern times, with our sophisticated scientific equipment, rain cannot be predicted more than a few hours in advance. Though rain appears to be a natural occurrence, due to its unpredictable nature it is deemed a Divine decree. Rabbi Kasher explains the Messianic Era in the same vein. It will appear to be a natural event; however, since it will be totally unpredictable, it must in actuality be a Divine decree.

Though the successes of the Bar Kokhba rebellion seemed to be a natural historical event, they were totally unexpected. An unknown messianic figure was able to push off the yoke of the mighty Roman Empire for two decades. Whole countries fell before Rome in a matter of weeks or months, yet Bar Kokhba wrestled Judea away from the tight grasp of the empire and gained military independence for many years. It is true there was no parting of the seas or affliction of plagues, but to the Jews, and even to the Romans, it must have seemed to be some Divine decree.

Another solution to the apparent contradiction is offered by the seventeenth-century kabbalist and biblical commentator, Rabbi Chaim ben Moshe ibn Atar. In his magnum opus, *Ohr HaChaim*, he qualifies the "natural theory."[9] Should the great merits of the Jewish People warrant an early arrival of the Messiah, the advent will be hailed with heavenly wonders. Should the Messiah have to wait until his proper time, his arrival will be through natural events.

31

Gog and Magog

In the Book of Ezekiel is the prophet's vision of the Messianic Era. In chapters 38 and 39, the prophet describes how the nations of the world will unite under the banner of Gog and Magog to wage war against Israel. Gog will be defeated and *"then they shall know that I am the Lord their God. . . . I will not hide My face from them any more, for I have poured out My spirit upon the House of Israel, saith the Lord"* (emphasis mine).

Who is Gog? Rashi says Gog is the name of a legendary king.[1] Rabbaynu Saadiah Goan refers to him as Ahromulus, after the legendary founder of Rome, Romulus.[2] Rabbaynu Saadiah says that Gog is descendant of the Edomite Romans. Malbim also identifies Gog as an Edomite.[3] Traditionally, Esau the Edomite, the brother of Jacob, was the ancestor of the Romans. Accordingly, it was quite understandable that Trajan and Hadrian, two emperors of Rome, could be construed as the personification of Gog.

Maharsha states that in the Messianic Era, there will be two Messiahs.[4] The Son of Joseph Messiah will lead the battle against the Edomites. That Messiah will be killed by the nations who joined the cause of the Edomites. The final victory will be obtained by the Son of David Messiah.

Abarnanel claims that Rebbe Akiva proclaimed Bar Kokhba to be the Messiah, but not the Son of David Messiah, rather the Son of Joseph Messiah.[5] However, there are several indications that Rebbe Akiva was claiming Bar Kokhba to be the Son of David Messiah. Rebbe Yochanan Tortah's rebuke to Rebbe Akiva was "Akiva, grass will sooner grow on your cheeks and the Son of David will not have come."[6] Rebbe Yochanan was certainly implying that Rebbe Akiva had called Bar Kokhba a son of David. Another indication, the fact the Sages tested Bar Kokhba to see if he could "smell the truth" would seem to indicate that Bar Kokhba claimed to be the son of David Messiah. Also, Maimonides states that Rebbe Akiva proclaimed him the "Messianic King."[7] The title of king could only be assumed by the Son of David Messiah.

Based on the evidence, it would seem to me that one of the two righteous brothers, Lulianus or Pappus, who instigated the Second Revolt against Trajan and were killed by Hadrian, would qualify as the Son of Joseph Messiah, and Rashi refers to them as "completely righteous."[8] Perhaps the Messiah, son of Joseph, could be two individuals, unlike the messianic king, son of David. In my opinion, Rebbe Akiva proclaimed Bar Kokhba to be the Son of David Messiah.

Who, or what, is Magog? Maharsha explains that Magog, as referred to in Ezekiel 38:2, is the name of the land over which Gog is king.[9] The Babylonian Talmud refers to the land of Magog as Kandia,[10] which Josephus says is Scythian,[11] a region centered north of the Black Sea in southeast Europe.

Ezekiel says that two nations occupy the land of Magog: Meshech and Tubal.[12] The Jerusalem Talmud[13] identifies the nation of Meshech with the Moscovites,[14] whereas Josephus calls them Cappadocians.[15]

The Talmud identifies Tubal as Unyaki.[16] The Jerusalem Talmud calls Tubal, Visinia.[17] Marcus Jastrow says that both

Unyaki and Visinia refer to the Roman province of Bithynia, an ancient district in northwest Asia Minor.

Radak says that the original connotations of the names of Meshech and Tubal have been forgotten.[18] The provinces that now bear these names are no indication as to the original context and meaning of these two places.

The Messiah's fight against Gog and the ensuing holocaust is to serve two purposes. First, it will serve as a purification process that will root out the wicked from among Mankind so that the surviving righteous can fulfill God's will on earth. Second, the miraculous salvation of the righteous will give evidence of the Messiah's divine mission so that all the nations of the world will accept him as their king.[19]

The focal point of the battle will be the domination of Israel, particularly Jerusalem. It will be a war against the Jews and the Jewish claim to sovereignty over Israel. Nations from all over the earth will unite under Gog to destroy the Jews and capture their land.[20]

Gog and his multitude of cohorts will make two attempts against Jerusalem and will not succeed. On the third try, however, Jerusalem will be captured.[21]

Rabbi Eliyahu Lapian relates in the name of Rabbi Elchanan Wasserman who said in the name of Choffetz Chaim that World War I was the first attempt of Gog. Choffetz Chaim also predicted that about twenty-five years after would occur a second world war, which would pale the first war.[22] Then will follow a third war, which will threaten the children of Jacob. May we be spared.

From the above, it is obvious that the war of Gog will be global in nature. Concerning the Bar Kokhba revolt, we have Dio Cassius's testimony that "many outside nations, too, were joining [the Romans] through eagerness for gain. The whole earth, one might almost say, was being stirred up over the matter."[23] The battle did, in fact, center over the conquest of Jerusalem, and in the end, Jerusalem fell.

After the fall of Jerusalem, the Messiah will miraculously lead his people to victory. According to the prophecy of Isaiah,[24] Gog will be killed by "the spirit of the mouth" of the Messiah.[25] Malbim[26] and Rabbi Moses Feinstein[27] say that in the end the Jews will not have to fight the invaders but rather God's miracles alone will destroy them as the verse says: *"I will rain upon him, and upon his bands, and upon the many people that are with him, an overflowing rain, great hailstones, fire, and brimstone. Thus I shall show My greatness and sanctify Myself and I will be known in the eyes of many nations. They shall know I am the Lord"* [28] (emphasis mine).

The dead will be so numerous that it will take seven months to bury the corpses.[29] Gog and his entourage will be buried east of the Sea of Kinneret.[30]

Will the Messiah be proclaimed before or after the war? There are three opinions:

1. Maimonides explains that the war of Gog and Israel will occur toward the beginning of the messianic era.[31] Chassam Sofer explains that the Messiah will be proclaimed first and that this will be followed by the war of Gog.[32]
2. Maharsha says that the Messiah will be proclaimed during the course of the war.[33]
3. Yefeh Tohar says that according to the order of the prayers in the Shemoneh Essray (Eighteen Benedictions), first will be the "sounding of the great horn" to signal the ingathering of the Jews of the Diaspora.[34] That will be followed by the war of Gog and Israel's plea for justice from the One "who loves righteousness and justice." That war will culminate in the arrival of "the scion of David."

Meiri and the *Seder HaDoros* say that the Bar Kokhba Era began during the reign of Trajan. According to Maimonides' view that the proclamation of the Messiah will precede the great war, Rebbe Akiva must have declared Bar Kokhba to be the Messiah before the Second Revolt, or circa 112 C.E. According to Maharsha, the proclamation is to be during the war, which would mean a few years after 112 C.E.

According to Yefeh Tohar, the proclamation of the Messiah is to be made after the Jews' plea for justice has been answered. That could have been during the reign of Hadrian when, to appease the Jews, he granted them permission to rebuild their Temple, circa 117 C.E.

32

The Prophet Elijah

The prophet Malachi foretold: *"Behold! I will send to you Elijah the prophet before the coming of the great and dreadful day of the Lord. He shall turn the hearts of the fathers to the children and the hearts of the children to the fathers, lest I come and smite the earth with a curse"* (emphasis mine).[1]

In Jewish lore, the coming of the Messiah is closely associated with the appearance of the Prophet Elijah. What will be the function of Elijah? There are many opinions:

1. To announce the coming of the Messiah.[2]
2. To anoint the Messiah as king.[3]
3. To bring about the repentance of Israel.[4]
4. To bring universal harmony and peace.[5]
5. To restore the treasures of the Jewish People that were hidden by Jeremiah before the destruction of the First Temple, namely, the Holy Ark, the flask of manna, the waters of purification, the oil of anointing, and the staff of Aaron.[6]
6. To resurrect the dead.[7]
7. To ordain the rabbis of the Sanhedrin.[8]
8. To clarify unresolved halachic disputes.[9]

Is Elijah to come before or after the revelation of the Messiah? There are three opinions:

1. Pesiktah states Elijah will come three days before the Messiah.
2. Ramban says Elijah will come on the day before the Messiah.[10]
3. Maimonides says that Elijah will come after the Messiah.[11] Chassam Sofer explains that Elijah will come after the Messiah, but before the day of the final battle of Gog and Magog.[12]

The first two opinions, that Elijah will come before the Messiah, do not seem to fit with the historical fact that Rebbe Akiva proclaimed Bar Kokhba the Messiah. There is no mention by any commentary that the Prophet Elijah appeared to announce or anoint Bar Kokhba. The events do conform with the opinion of Maimonides that Elijah will appear only after the announcement of the divinely appointed Messiah.

33

The Messianic Era

The Talmud says, "There will be no difference between the world as it exists today and the days of the Messiah except for government rule."[1] The Talmud is stating that the major distinction of the Messianic Era will be political. Today, every nation works to achieve its own end. Each seeks to be an independent political entity. Independence requires natural resources, for without them, one must depend on other nations. If the natural resources are not available, wealth must be accumulated to buy them. And there is always the possibility that the other nations will impose unreasonable conditions or even refuse to sell their products. Many wars have been fought over these economic factors.

Some nations take pride in their culture or philosophical doctrines. They seek to impose their beliefs on others. Many wars have been fought over culture, religion, and philosophy.

The Messianic Era will herald the onset of a single, universal political system, with the Messiah at its helm. There will no longer be localized concern over natural resources. The spprit of universal cooperation and brotherhood will reign supreme. There will no longer be the need to accumulate wealth. There will no longer be diverse cultures and philosophies. Just as in the very beginning of time, a single man was created, so, too, in the end of days, all Mankind will unite as a single entity. There will no longer be the need for war.

> *And it shall come to pass in the last days . . . they shall beat their swords into plowshares and their spears into pruning-hooks. Nation shall not lift up sword against nation, neither shall they learn war any more* (emphasis mine).[2]

History has taught us that in a world divided into various nations, no nation can achieve eternal independence or perpetual self-reliance. The nation must eventually conquer or be conquered. But in a one-world political entity, true independence can be achieved. Man can turn his focus to the realm of the spirit and strive for moral perfection and intellectual excellence.[3] The Messianic Era will usher in the rebirth of virtue, a renaissance of spirituality, and an understanding of God's will.[4] The world will experience a spiritual revival that will result in the perfection of the human condition. Man will achieve the same state of godliness as on the day he was created.[5]

> *For the earth shall be full of the knowledge of the Lord, as the waters cover the sea* (emphasis mine).[6] So will be the enlightenment in the future to come, not only for Israel, but for all the nations of the world.[7]

> *The wolf also shall dwell with the lamb, the leopard shall lie down with the kid, and the calf and the young lion and the fatling together, and a little child shall lead them* (emphasis mine).[8]

Maimonides assumes this verse to be allegorical.[9] It depicts the relationship of Israel and the nations of the world. The verse is vividly portraying the state of harmony and tranquillity that will be achieved in the Messianic Era. However, Ramban takes the verse to be literal.[10] Just as former enemy nations will be at peace, so, too, will the former enemies of the animal kingdom peacefully coexist.

There are ten opinions quoted in the Talmud as to the duration of the Messianic Era:

1. Rebbe Eliezer—the Messianic Era will last 40 years.[11]
2. Rebbe Elazer ben Azariah—the Messianic Era will last seventy years.[12]
3. Rebbe Yehudah HaNasi—the Messianic Era will last three generations.[13]
4. Rebbe Yehudah HaNasi—the Messianic Era will last 365 years.[14]
5. Rebbe Dosah—the Messianic Era will last 400 years.[15]
6. Tanna Divai Eliyahu—the Messianic Era will last 2,000 years.[16]
7. Rav Nachman bar Yitzchok—the Messianic Era will last as many years as from the time of the Flood until the Messiah's arrival.[17]
8. Shmuel—the Messianic Era will last as many years as from Creation until his arrival.[18]
9. Avimi brei di'Rebbe Avohu—the Messianic Era will last 7,000 years.[19]
10. Rebbe Yehudah HaNasi—the Messianic Era will last 365,000 years.[20]

It is interesting to note that Rebbe Yehudah HaNasi gave two different opinions as to the duration of the Messianic Era: three generations and either 365 or 365,000 years. Could it be that the "three generations" refers to Bar Kokhba, which according to Meiri and *Seder HaDoros* lasted for three generations? Did Rebbe Yehudah mean to imply that there would be two Messiahs? One of the Messiahs would be a glimmer of hope in order to instill the feasibility of the dream for future generations. That glimmer of hope would last for three generations. The realization of that hope would come in the end of days and last for either 365 or 365,000 years.

34

The Resurrection of
the Dead

*"And many of them that sleep in the dust of the earth shall awake,
some to everlasting life, some to shame and everlasting contempt."*[1]

"Fortunate is he that waiteth."[2]

The Prophet Daniel is making reference here to the
Resurrection of the Dead in the days to come. Maimonides lists this belief among the thirteen principals
of faith of Jewish doctrine.

Ritvah explains that there will be two periods of resurrection.[3] One will occur near the beginning of the Messianic Era.
That resurrection will be for those who had eagerly awaited
the coming of the Messiah. This is the resurrection to which
Daniel refers when he says, "Fortunate is he that waiteth."
Another, more general resurrection will occur later, on Judgment Day.

Radvaz explains the view of Ritva to mean that the first
resurrection will be a unification of the body and soul in order
that the righteous may enjoy the glory of the Jewish People and
the Temple.[4] The second resurrection will occur in the sixth
millennia of the creation and will be a resurrection of the soul.

Radvaz maintains that the second resurrection will be spiritual and not physical. Maimonides and Ramban indicate that the resurrection will be a unification of the body and soul. Maimonides states that after the Resurrection Era, which may last many thousands of years, the soul will depart for its eternal reward.[5] Ramban, however, maintains that body and soul shall remain bound together forever.[6]

Earlier we mentioned the various opinions as to the length of years of the Messianic Era, which range from 40 to 365,000 years. All the opinions do agree that the Resurrection will occur at the end of the Messianic Era; therefore, those who say the era will be of a short duration are not attempting to diminish the reward of the righteous but rather, in effect, are saying that the reward of resurrection will occur earlier.[7]

The opinion that there will be a Resurrection also at the beginning of the Messianic Era is difficult to reconcile with the historic events of Rebbe Akiva and Bar Kokhba. It is important to note that Ritva says that the opinion of Shmuel is that there will not be any resurrection in the beginning of the Messianic Era, but only at the end.[8] Perhaps Rebbe Akiva was in accordance with the view later espoused by Shmuel.

35

The Messianic Temple

And it shall come to pass in the end of days that the mountain of the Lord's house shall be established at the head of the mountains and exalted from among the hills. Many nations will go and say "Come let us go up to the mountain of the lord, to the house of the God of Jacob." (emphasis mine).[1]

The verse tells that in the Messianic Era there will be a temple rebuilt on the Temple Mount. Whether the building of the Temple will precede the arrival of the Messiah or if it will be built after his arrival is a matter of dispute.

The Jerusalem Talmud states quite clearly, in the name of Rebbe Achah, that the Temple will be built before the arrival of the Messiah.[2] Rashi seems to support this view.[3] However, Maimonides maintains that the Temple will be rebuilt after the coming of the Messiah.[4]

In preceding chapters we have had much discussion concerning the possibility that Bar Kokhba did, in fact, build a temple.

36

Rebbe Hillel's Messiah

One of the most perplexing quotes concerning the Messiah is found in the Talmud:

> Rebbe Hillel said, "There shall be no Messiah for Israel; they have already benefited from him in the days of Hezikiah." Rav Yosef said, "May the Master forgive Rebbe Hillel [for saying that]. When did Hezikiah live? During the [time of] the First Temple. Yet, the prophet Zechariah prophesied in the days of the Second Temple saying 'Rejoice greatly, daughter of Zion, shout forth, daughter of Zion, behold the King cometh unto thee. He is righteous and he is the savior, humble, riding upon an ass.' "[1]

The identity of Rebbe Hillel is not known. He certainly was considered one of the Sages since he is referred to as "rebbe." He seems to have been a contemporary of Rav Yosef, who lived more than a century after the Bar Kokhba epoch. Taken at face value, it appears that Rebbe Hillel did not believe in the concept of a messianic savior. Yet belief in the coming of the

Messiah is one of the Thirteen Principles of Faith, as enumerated by Maimonides. Besides this one comment by Rebbe Hillel, nowhere in the Talmud or any of the commentaries do we find any doubt as to the validity and significance of the messianic principle. Could it have been that the Bar Kokhba debacle caused Rebbe Hillel to abandon faith in the coming of the Messiah? The twelfth-century Spanish commentator, Rabbi Meir HaLevi Abulafia (Yad Ramah, Sanhedrin), certainly felt Rebbe Hillel had despaired of all hope.

The other commentaries take a different approach and attempt to explain Rebbe Hillel's statement to conform with the Messianic Principle. First and foremost among the commentaries is Rashi. He explains that Rebbe Hillel certainly believed in the coming of the Messianic Era. However, he did not believe that the era will be heralded by a messianic man but rather that only God Himself can bring human history to its proper climax and spiritual destiny.

Rabbi Yosef Albo (Ikrim), the fifteenth-century Spanish philosopher, suggests that perhaps Rebbe Hillel meant that the prophesy of Zechariah could be a figurative vision referring to God. The verse alone does not compel a literal interpretation. However, Rebbe Hillel did agree that the Messiah would be a man. He based that belief on rabbinic tradition rather than scriptural interpretation.

One of Nachmanides' students, Rabbi David Bonvoir, assumes that Rebbe Hillel thought the onset of the Messianic Era would be so closely followed by the rebirth of Mankind during the Resurrection of the Dead that there would be little purpose to the Messianic Era.

Rabbi Shem Tov ibn Shaprut (Pardes Rimonim) explains that the Messiah will only come because of our merits. He will not come as a debt to the merits of our forefathers. That debt was repaid during the magnificent reign of Hezekiah.

Rabbi Menachem Kasher (Tekufah HaGedolah) proposes another explanation for Rebbe Hillel's perplexing comment.

The Talmud mentions two messiahs, the Messiah, son of Joseph, and the Messiah, son of David.[2] The Messiah, son of Joseph, will begin the military aspect of the Messianic Era. Later, the Messiah, son of David, will complete the task and be hailed as King of the Jews. The reason why two Messiahs will be required relates to the division of the First Temple of Israel into two political entities—Judah and Israel. Ten tribes occupied the northern portion of the country and established their own king, who was a descendant of Joseph. This state was called Israel. Two tribes occupied the southern portion of the country. They had their own king, a descendant of King David. This state was called Judah.

The Ten Tribes of the north were exiled from their land by the Assyrians. The district of Judah was later exiled by the Babylonians. In the days to come, the Messiah, son of Joseph, will be responsible for the ingathering of the Ten Tribes of Israel. The Messiah, son of David, will be responsible for the ingathering of the two southern tribes. This idea was first presented by Rabbi Moses Schreiber in the nineteenth century.[3]

Rabbi Kasher points out that Rebbe Akiva contends that the Ten Tribes will never return to the fold of the Children of Israel because of their lack of merit.[4] Accordingly, there will be no need for a Messiah, son of Joseph. Perhaps when Rebbe Hillel said that there were will be no Messiah for Israel, he meant that there will be no Messiah, son of Joseph, for the Ten Tribes of the district called Israel.

Rabbi Kasher's contention solves two dilemmas. During the Bar Kokhba revolution there was no mention of a Messiah, son of Joseph, but only of one Messiah, presumably the Messiah, son of David. Maimonides, in his codes and writings, likewise makes no mention of the Messiah, son of Joseph. The Bar Kokhba revolution was supported by Rebbe Akiva. According to the view of Rabbi Kasher, Rebbe Akiva maintained there would be no Messiah, son of Joseph. The absence of such a historical figure would not present a problem to Rebbe Akiva. We could also speculate that Maimonides upheld the view of Rebbe Akiva and therefore made no mention of Messiah, son of Joseph.

However, the very text of the Talmud does not seem to support Rabbi Kasher's view. After quoting Rebbe Hillel, the Talmud states:

> Rav Yosef said, "May the Master forgive Rebbe Hillel [for saying that]. When did Hezikiah live? During the [time of] the First Temple. Yet, the prophet Zechariah prophesied in the days of the Second Temple saying 'Rejoice greatly, daughter of Zion, shout forth, daughter of Zion, behold the King cometh unto thee. He is righteous and he is the savior, humble, riding upon an ass.' "[5]

Rav Yosef certainly understood Rebbe Hillel to refer to the Messiah, son of David, as indicated by the verse quoted here. Are we to understand that, according to Rabbi Kasher's contention, Rav Yosef's harsh comments were made based on a misunderstanding?

In the chapter entitled "Gog and Magog" (Chapter 31), I have suggested that one of the brothers Lulianus and Pappus, who lived during the Bar Kokhba epoch, may have been the Messiah, son of Joseph.

37

Was Rebbe Akiva Wrong?

T he question is often asked whether Rebbe Akiva erred in recognizing Bar Kokhba as the Messiah. To be sure, there were Snges, such as Rebbe Yochanan Tortah, who did not believe Bar Kokhba to be the Messiah, and in the end their view was borne out. But does that make Rebbe Akiva wrong?

Maimonides states:

> If there arises a king from the House of David, versed in Torah and performs the commandments like David his ancestor, according to the Written Law and according to the Oral Law, and compels all Israel to go in its ways to uphold it, and wages a war of God, it is *assumed* that he is the Messiah. If he successfully does this and builds the Temple in its proper place and gathers the dispersed of Israel, behold, he is *certainly* the Messiah (emphasis mine).[1]

Maimonides divides the qualifications of the Messiah into two states. The first state is the "assumed" Messiah. To qualify for the state, the Messiah must be a righteous descendant of King David who successfully wages a holy war. The second state is the "certain" Messiah. To qualify for this higher status, the Messiah must rebuild the Temple and gather the Jews of the Diaspora into Israel.

The term "assumed" (in Hebrew, "chezkas" or "chazakah") is a legal term. Often in judicial matters there is no clear evidence. A judge or rabbi is then obligated to follow certain guidelines, which are often based on assumptions. These guidelines are called "chazakah" and predetermine or influence the verdict.

For example, suppose a man is on trial for murder. The defendant claims that the victim was suffering a heart attack at the time of the murder and was in the process of dying. There is no medical evidence to back this contention. "Chazakah" dictates that without any substantiating evidence, the court may not take into consideration the defendant's claim. They must assume the victim was in a healthy state at the time of the murder. These "chazakah" guidelines are not considered absolute proof or verification of fact, but merely rules of judicial conduct.

If subsequently, evidence does surface that contradicts the halachic guidelines, the ruling will be changed. However, the judge or rabbi was not in error, for he merely followed the proper "chazakah" guidelines at the time when he had to render his verdict.

Maimonides gave very specific guidelines as to when to assume that a claim of Messiah may be rendered legitimate. Rebbe Akiva maintained that Bar Kokhba certainly met these requirements and therefore could legally be "assumed" to be the Messiah. Whether Bar Kokhba was in fact the Messiah, Rebbe Akiva could not know. He was merely following the proper code of halachic jurisprudence.

Was Rebbe Akiva wrong? He was not. Was Rebbe Akiva correct? Though his decision was legally correct, in actuality he was not. Perhaps, as speculated earlier, it was part of the Divine plan. The Diaspora has been in process for almost two thousand years. There have been many holocausts and countless expulsions. Through torture and forced conversions, through death marches and gas chambers, the Jew has steadfastly held onto his belief that one day, his lot would be better, that one day, Mankind would be better off. One day, the Messiah would come.

What enabled the Jewish People to keep such an almost incomprehensible hope alive—the hope that one day a savior would come and deliver them from the cruel inhumanities of their oppressors? It was Bar Kokhba. Bar Kokhba turned the small, defeated Jewish nation into a mighty force that, for a short while, pushed back the mightiest empire the world has ever known. Bar Kokhba was a glimpse into the future, a glimpse that enabled the Jews to know that one day, the Messiah will truly come.

38

Maimonides' Doctrine of the Messiah

M uch of this work has been drawn from the wellsprings of the classic Judaic philosopher, codifier, and commentator, Rabbi Moses Maimonides. His views concerning the Messiah and his era are primarily found in his "Laws of Royalty," chapters 11 and 12, and in his "Letter to Yemen."

LAWS OF ROYALTY

Chapter 11, Paragraph 1

In the future, the Messianic King will arise[1] and restore the House of David to its former dominion.[2] He will build the Temple and gather the dispersed of Israel.[3] Justice will be revived in his days as it was in former times.[4] Sacrifices will be offered. Sabbatical years[5] and Jubilees will be kept, as will all the commandments in the Torah.

Those who do not believe in his coming and those who do not await his arrival, not only do they reject the prophets, but also the Torah of Moses our teacher. Concerning [the Messiah], the Torah testifies "The Lord thy God will return thy captives and have compassion upon thee. He will return and gather thee from among all the nations that the Lord your God has scattered you there." (Deuteronomy 30:3-5) This concept, expressed clearly in the Torah, encompasses all the words spoken by the prophets.

Similarly, in the portion of [the Torah concerning] Bilaam it is stated: ["I see him, but not now. I behold him, but not soon. A star shall shoot forth from Jacob and a scepter shall arise from Israel. He shall smite the ends of Moab and dig up the sons of Seth. Edom shall be a possession and he will possess Seir, the enemy. Israel will show strength" (Numbers 24:17-18)].

[Bilaam] prophesies about two saviors. The first savior is [King] David who saved Israel from their enemies. A later savior will arise from his descendants and save Israel. "I see him, but not now" refers to David. "I behold him, but not close" refers to the Messianic King.

"A star shall shoot forth from Jacob" refers to David. "And a scepter shall arise from Israel" refers to the Messianic King.

"He shall smite the ends of Moab" refers to David, and so it is written "And he smote Moab." (2 Samuel 8:2) "And dig up the sons of Seth" refers to the Messianic King, as it says (in the prophecy of Zachariah) "He shall rule from sea to sea." (Zechariah 9:10)

"Edom shall be a possession" refers to David, as it is written "And Edom became slaves to David." (2 Samuel 8:6) "He will possess Seir, the enemy" refers to the Messianic King, as it is written (in the prophecy of Obadiah), "And the saviors shall go up on Mount Zion to judge Mount Essau, and the kingdom shall be God's." (Obadiah 1:21)

Chapter 11, Paragraph 2

[Another biblical indication of the Messianic Era is] also [found in the portion of] the cities of refuge. It states: "And when the Lord your God widens thy boundaries . . . thou shall add three more cities [of refuge]." (Deuteronomy 19:8–9). This never came about and [we know that] God does not command hollow words. Indications [of the Messianic Era] from the words of the prophets are not necessary, for their books are replete in this matter.

Chapter 11, Paragraph 3

Let it not enter your mind that the Messianic King will be required to perform signs and miracles, declare revelation or revive the dead, or matters similar to these. This is not so. Rebbe Akiva, the great sage from among the wise men of the Mishna, supported the monarch Bar Kokhba. [Rebbe Akiva] proclaimed him to be the Messianic King. So it seemed to [Rebbe Akiva] and all the wise men of his generation. [Bar Kokhba] was [recognized] as the Messianic King until he was killed because of his sins. When he was killed, it was realized that he was not [the Messiah].

The Sages did not require of [Bar Kokhba] any sign or miracle.[6] The essence of these matters is that the Torah, its regulations and laws, are eternal. We cannot add to it nor diminish from it.[7]

Chapter 11, Paragraph 4

Should there arise a king from the house of David, steeped in the Torah and performs its commandments[8] like David his ancestor, following the Written Torah and the Oral Torah, and should he compel all Israel to follow in its ways, and strengthen its minutest detail, and wage a holy war, behold, this [man] is assumed to be the Messiah.

If he is successful and rebuilds the Temple in its [proper] place[9] and gathers the dispersed of Israel, he is certainly the Messiah.

[The following paragraphs are omitted in many editions of Maimonides' Code because the papal censors deemed them offensive.]

Should he not succeed in these matters or should he be killed, it is understood that he was not the Messiah promised by the Torah. He is regarded like the other kings from the House of David who were perfect and fit, who also died. God sent him to test the public, as it says "Some of the intelligent will stumble, to make a purification among them, to choose and cleanse them until the end of time, for it is yet that appointed time." (Dan. 11:35)

The Christian savior, who was thought to be the Messiah, was killed by the court. Daniel prophesied concerning him "In that time many will arise against the king of the south, also the rebellious sons of thy people will raise themselves up to establish the vision, but they will stumble." (Dan. 11:14)

There is no greater stumbling block than [a false Messiah]. The prophets spoke of a redeemer for Israel who will save them and gather the remnants and strengthen the commandments. The [false Messiah] causes Israel to be slain by the sword, to scatter those who remain, and to humiliate them. He abolishes the Torah and deceives most of the world to serve a deity other than God.

The plans of the Creator of the Universe cannot be fathomed by man. His ways are not like our ways and His thoughts are not like our thoughts.[10] All of the [above] things were caused by the Christian savior and the Moslem prophet who arose afterwards. All of this was to straighten the way for the [true] Messianic King and to prepare the world to serve God in harmony.

Chapter 12, Paragraph 1

Do not think that in the Messianic Era the nature of the world will change or that a new creation will appear. Rather, the

nature of the world will be as before. That which is written in
Isaiah (11:6) "The wolf shall live with the sheep and the leopard
will lie with the kid" is only a metaphor and allegory.[11] It
signifies that Israel will dwell in safety with the [former] evil
rulers of the nations, who are compared to a wolf and leopard.
So it is written (Jeremiah 5:6) "Therefore slayeth them—the
lion from the forest, the wolf of the deserts. Waste them, the
leopard that lies in wait against the cities."

[The enemies of Israel] shall all be turned to the true religion. They will no longer steal or destroy. They shall partake
only that which is permitted[12] and [dwell] in tranquility with
Israel. It is written (Isaiah 11:7) "The lion like the cattle will
consume hay."

All similar expressions [in the prophets] concerning the
Messiah are parables. In the Messianic Era it will become
revealed to what the parable refers and to which matter is
hinted.

Chapter 12, Paragraph 2

The Sages have said: There is no difference between this world
and the Messianic Era other than subjugation to the government.

The words of the prophets, taken at face value, indicate that
the war of Gog and Magog will be at the beginning of the
Messianic Era. Before the war, a prophet will arise to correct
Israel and prepare their hearts. So it is written (Malachi 3:23)
"Behold! I am sending unto you the prophet Elijah before the
day of the coming of the Lord."

Elijah will not come to declare impure that which is pure or
to declare pure that which is impure. He will not render unfit
those men who are assumed to be fit or render fit those who
are assumed to be unfit. He will only come to instill peace in
the world, as it is written (Malachi 3:24) "He shall turn back the
heart of the fathers to their sons and the heart of the sons to
their fathers, lest I come and smite the earth with a curse."

Some Sages say that Elijah will come before the arrival of the Messiah. However, all these matters, and similar issues, are not known exactly how they will happen. The words of the prophets are closed and the Sages have no tradition other than the decision of legal experts. Therefore, there are differences of opinion concerning these matters. In any event, the sequence of future events and their details are not fundamental principles of faith. It is best not to delve into these matters nor to elaborate on the midrashic texts concerning these matters. They should not be regarded a primary importance, for they do not bring awe or love. One should not try to calculate the End of Days.

Our Sages have said: Blasted are the bones of those who calculate the end. One should await and have faith that [the Messiah] will come.

Chapter 12, Paragraph 3

In the days of the Messianic King, when his kingdom is firmly established, all Israel will gather before him. He will establish their lineage through the holy spirit which will rest upon him. So it is written (Malachi 3:3) "He will sit as a melter and purifier of silver; he will purify the sons of Levi and refine them like gold and silver."

The sons of Levi will be purified first. He will say "This is a priest and this one is a Levite." He will push away those who are not true Israelites, as it is written (Ezra 2:63) "And the [prophet] said unto them that they should not eat of the sacred things until there arises a priest with the prophetic breastplate [Urim and Tummim]." This implies that with the holy spirit lineage will be established. He will only establish the tribal lineage of every Jew and reveal from which tribe they belong. He will not declare anyone to be of illegitimate birth or descendant of a slave, for the law is that [illegitimate Jews] who have assimilated into the fold are assimilated.

Chapter 12, Paragraph 4

Our Sages and prophets have not desired the Messianic Era so
they could rule the world, overpower the nations, and elevate
themselves from among the peoples. They did not [desire the
Messiah] so they could eat, drink, and be merry. They [desired
him] so they would be free to [devote themselves to] the Torah
and its wisdom. [They desired him to abolish] all oppressors
[of the Jews] and [those who sought to] abolish [the Torah], so
they would be worthy of an everlasting life in the World to
Come, as we have already explained in the [section of the]
Laws of Repentance.

Chapter 12, Paragraph 5

In the [Messianic] Era there will be no hunger or war, no
jealousy or rivalry, for goodness will flow plentifully and the
delights will be found [in abundance] like the dust. The sole
occupation of mankind will be to know God. Therefore, Israel
will become great sages and know the hidden things and
comprehend the intent of their Creator, according to the [lim-
ited] ability of man. So it is written (Isaiah 11:9) "The land will
be full of knowledge of God, as the waters cover the oceans."

EXCERPTS FROM MAIMONIDES' "LETTER TO YEMEN"

Basically you must realize that the true time of the End of Days
is impossible for anyone to ever know. As Daniel explained,
"Closed and sealed are these matters until the end of days."
(Daniel 12:9) Though some sages gave much thought concerning these matters, the prophet predicted this and said, "Many
will go afar and opinions will be many." (Daniel 12:4) He
means to say that many opinions and arguments [will be
proposed regarding the time of the arrival of the Messiah].

God has informed us through His prophets that some men will calculate the end of [the exile when the] Messiah [will come]. The date will pass unfulfilled. We are cautioned from having doubts [if the Messiah will ever arrive]. [The Prophets] say that you should not despair if your calculation does not come to fruition. The longer [Messiah] delays, the more intensely we should hope. So it says (Habakkuk 2:3) "There is yet to be a vision for the set time, one that states the end and is not false. Though he tarries, wait for him. He will surely come without delay."

The end of the Egyptian Exile was foretold by God [to Abraham]: "And they shall be enslaved and oppressed for four hundred years" (Genesis 15:13). Still, the exact time was not known and many uncertainties arose. Some thought the four hundred years began when Jacob came down to Egypt. Others thought [the four hundred years began] when the enslavement began, which was seventy years after Jacob came down to Egypt. Still others thought it began when the prophecy [of four hundred years] was revealed to our father Abraham. When four hundred years elapsed from the revelation of the prophecy, some Jews [from the tribe of Ephraim] left Egypt. This was thirty years before Moses [appeared before the Jews]. [The Tribe of Ephraim] thought the end [of the Exile] had come. [In the end, many Israelites from the Tribe of Ephraim] were killed by the Egyptians and the enslavement was made even harsher. Our Sages of blessed memory have explained the words of David (Psalms 78:9) "The archers of Ephraim were overturned on the day of approach" to refer to those men who erred in their calculations and thought the time of the exodus had arrived.

The correct date was four hundred years after the birth of Isaac, the son of Abraham. As it says (Genesis 21:12) "For Isaac will be called your descendant," and God had declared "Your descendants will be a stranger in a land which is not theirs, and they will be enslaved and oppressed for four hundred years." (Genesis 15:13)

During that exile, the [Egyptians] ruled over [the Israelites] and enslaved them and made them weary. The correct interpretation of the verse is that the four hundred years will be a time of dwelling [in a land in which the Israelites will be regarded] as strangers. It did not mean [to imply that all four hundred years will be years] of enslavement.

This was not known until the great prophet [Moses] arose and it was realized that from the birth of Isaac until the Exodus from Egypt was four hundred years.

You must certainly [now] understand that if the [duration of the Egyptian exile], which was known [beforehand], created so much uncertainty, how much more so the end of this exile. The great length of this exile has caused the prophets to fear and tremble to the extent that one of them declared "Forever will You be angry with us, prolonging Your anger generation after generation." (Psalms 85:6) Isaiah said, regarding the great length of this exile, "They shall be gathered in a pit as prisoners; they shall be fenced in a corral. After many days shall they be remembered." (Isaiah 24:22)

Daniel predicted the great depths of the knowledge of the End of Days, that it is closed and sealed. Therefore our Sages of blessed memory have prevented us from attempting to calculate the end when the Messiah will arrive in order not to cause the people to err and despair should the [predicted] end come and he does not arrive. The Sages of blessed memory have said (Sanhedrin 97b) "Blasted are the bones of those who calculated the end." It is a stumbling block for the masses. Therefore, the Sages prayed that the minds [of those who attempted to calculate] will become confused and the calculation will be in error [so that no one will regard them seriously].

When will the Messiah arise and where will he [initially] appear? First, he will appear in the Land of Israel, for in the Land of Israel will be the revelation. As it is written (Mal. 3:1) "Suddenly he will come to his Temple, the master whom you seek. The messenger of the covenant whom you desire. Be-

hold! He is coming saith the Lord of Hosts." However, the
manner in which he will arise, you should realize, is not
known before it will happen. It cannot be said beforehand that
he is the son of so-and-so, from a certain family. An unknown
man will arise before his identity [is revealed] and the signs
and wonders that will be seen through his hand, they will
prove his true claim.[13] So God said to us when He spoke
regarding this matter "Behold! A man called Tzemach [growth]
will grow himself, [he will not require others to endorse his
elevated position]." (Zechariah 6:12)

Isaiah, likewise said that he will appear an unknown [be-
forehand] regarding his father, mother, and family. "He shot
up like a sapling, like a root out of dry land." (Isaiah 53:2)

After appearing in the "land of desire" [Israel, see Ezekiel
20:6], and [after] gathering all the Jews into Jerusalem and
other cities, the word will spread east and west until it reaches
you in the land of Yemen and to the inhabitants beyond in the
land of India. So it was written by the hand of Isaiah, "Go
swiftly messengers." (Isaiah 18:2)

The general qualities [of the Messiah] that were told by the
prophets, beginning with our teacher, Moses, and ending
with [the prophet] Malachi, you can gather them from the
twenty-four books [of the T'nach, or Bible]. The outstanding
quality that is attributed to [the Messiah] is that when his
identity is revealed, the kings of the land will tremble when
they hear of it; they will fear and shake, and their kingdoms
will plot how to stand against him, by the sword or other
means. However, they will not succeed in any claim or com-
plaint against him. They will be unable to deny his claim. They
will tremble on account of the wonders that will be brought
through his hand. Their hands will be upon their mouths.

So said Isaiah telling of the time when the kings will hear of
him "On his account many nations will jump, at him kings will
close their mouth . . ." (Isaiah 52:15). Furthermore, [Isaiah]
said that the very word [of the Messiah] will kill those he

wishes. None can escape or save himself from him. So it says "He will strike the land by the rod of his mouth; with the breath of his lips he will slay the wicked." (Isaiah 11:4)

The abolition of destruction and war from the east until the west will not come at the beginning of his revelation. That will occur after the war of Gog and Magog as explained by Ezekiel, of blessed memory.

Notes

CHAPTER 2

1. Eichah Rabah 2:4.
2. Haggai 2:6.
3. Sanhedrin 97b.
4. Numbers 24:17; Rashi and Ramban ad loc. explain the verse to refer to the Messiah.
5. Rambam Hilchos Milochim 11:3.
6. Yerushalmi Taanis 4:5.
7. Ibid.
8. Ibid.
9. Korbon Ha Eidah, ibid.
10. Eichah Rabah 2:7.

CHAPTER 3

1. *History of the Jews.*
2. Eichah Rabah 1:45.

CHAPTER 4

1. Berayshis Rabah 64:10.
2. Ibid.
3. Ibid.
4. Rashi Taanis 18b.

CHAPTER 5

1. Berayshis Rabah 77:3.
2. Me'ilah 17a.

CHAPTER 6

1. Eichah Rabah 1:16.
2. Yerushalmi Taanis 4:5.
3. Rambam Taanis 5:3.
4. Yerushalmi Taanis 4:5.

CHAPTER 7

1. Eichah Rabah 3:9.
2. Eichah Rabah 2:4; Yerushalmi Taanis 4:5.
3. Ibid.
4. Ibid.
5. Sanhedrin 93b.
6. Eichah Rabah 2:4; Yerushalmi Taanis 4:5.
7. Rambam Taanis 5:3.
8. Mishna Taanis 4:6.
9. Eichah Rabah 3:9.
10. Ibid. 1:16.

CHAPTER 8

1. *Roman History* 69:12–14.
2. *Bar Kokhba,* p. 258.
3. Me'ilah 17a.
4. Doros HaRishonim 4:27.
5. *Bar Kokhba,* p. 257.
6. Ibid.
7. Ibid.

CHAPTER 11

1. *Bar Kokhba,* p. 129.
2. Sucah 34b.
3. *Bar Kokhba,* p. 130.
4. Ibid., p. 132.
5. Ibid., p. 133.

CHAPTER 12

1. Eichah 1:16.

CHAPTER 14

1. Numbers 15:38.
2. Menachos 9:6.
3. Menachos 43a.

CHAPTER 15

1. *Naturalis Historia* 5:73.
2. *Wars*, bk. 2, ch. 8.

CHAPTER 16

1. Avos D'Rebbe Nosson 5:2.
2. Rosh HaShana 2:2.
3. Leviticus 23:5–16.
4. *The Temple Scroll*, p. 97.
5. Rosh HaShana 2:1.

CHAPTER 17

1. Sanhedrin 93b.
2. Ibid.
3. Ibid.
4. Ibid.

CHAPTER 18

1. Melochim 11:4.
2. Pesachim 74a.
3. Rashash, Pesachim 74a.
4. Baba Kama 97b.
5. Sanhedrin 11b.
6. Avodah Zora 52b; Bechoros 50a.
7. *Sibylinne Oracles*, bk. V, p. 555, Perry's translation.
8. Shemos Rabah 51:5.
9. Divorim Rabah 3:13.
10. *History of the Jews.*

11. Chullin 11b, 12a.
12. Ibid. 12a.
13. Taanis, ch. 5, rule 3.
14. Pesachim 3b.
15. Ibid.
16. See Doros HaRishonim, p. 681.
17. Nedarim 23a.
18. Eruchin 27a.

CHAPTER 19

1. Midos 2:1.
2. Midos 5:1.
3. *Bais HaBechirah* 5:3.

CHAPTER 20

1. *History of the Jews.*
2. Sucah 41a.
3. *Bais HaBechirah* 1:1.
4. Assay 20; Soresh 3.
5. Minchas Chinuch 95.
6. *Bais HaLevi,* end of vol. 2, Sermon 16.
7. Sucah 41a.
8. Baba Kama 97b.
9. Baba Basra 3b.

CHAPTER 21

1. Introduction to Avos, p. 29.
2. *Seder HaDoros* 1:159, yr. 3880, quoting Zemach Dovid.
3. Taanis 4:5.

CHAPTER 22

1. Taanis 29a.
2. Taanis 4:5.
3. Doros HaRishonim 4:31.
4. Sanhedrin 93b.
5. Taanis 4:5.
6. Sanhedrin 97b.
7. Doros HaRishonim, 4:31, quoting Shere, p. 767.

CHAPTER 25

1. Berochos 1:4.
2. Genesis 49:26.
3. Ibid.

CHAPTER 26

1. *Ecclesiastical History,* ch. 4.
2. *Apology,* bk. 1, ch. 47.
3. *Answer to the Jews,* ch. 13.

CHAPTER 28

1. Isaiah 11:2.
2. Bartenurah, Commentary to Ruth, Chassam Sofer Likutim no. 88.
3. Sanhedrin 88b.
4. Isaiah, para. 499.
5. Toldos 14.
6. Deuteronomy 34:10.
7. Yaaros Devash II,2.

8. Teshuva 9:2.
9. Maimonides, Melochim 12:3.
10. Isaiah II:2,3.
11. Sanhedrin 93b.
12. Melochim 11:3.
13. Baba Metzia 59b.

CHAPTER 29

1. From Sanhedrin 98a.
2. Sanhedrin 97b; Rashi ad loc.
3. Sanhedrin 97b; Rashi ad loc.
4. Sanhedrin 97b; Rashi ad loc.
5. Sanhedrin 97b.
6. Ibid.
7. Ibid. 97a.
8. Ibid. 97b.
9. Mayona HaKetz 1:2.
10. Sefer HeGeulah 4.
11. Letter to Yemen; Introduction to Mishna, Sanhedrin, ch. 10.
12. Daniel 12:4.
13. Sanhedrin 98a.
14. Ibid. 97a.
15. Ibid. 98a.
16. Ibid.
17. Ibid. 97a.
18. Ibid.
19. Ibid.
20. Ibid.
21. Ibid.
22. Ibid. 98a.
23. Ibid. 98b.
24. Ibid.

CHAPTER 30

1. *Seder HaYom.*
2. Commentary to Song of Songs 8:13.
3. Commentary to Psalms 146:3.
4. *Shem Olam,* ch. 14.
5. Yalkut Shimoni Chron. II 31:35.
6. Tanchumah Lev. 12.
7. Midrash Psalms 107:2.
8. Eichah Zutah 1:28.
9. *Ohr HaChaim,* Numbers 24:17.

CHAPTER 31

1. Ezekiel 38:2.
2. Commentary to Daniel, ch. 11.
3. Zechariah 12:2.
4. Sucah 52a.
5. Yehuos Mesicho 2:4.
6. Jer. Tal. Taanis 4:5.
7. Melochim 11:3.
8. Taanis 18b.
9. Yoma 10a.
10. Ibid.
11. *Antiquities* 1:6.
12. Ezekiel 38:2.
13. Megilah 1:9.
14. According to Pnai Moshe in Jer. Tal.
15. *Antiquities* 1:6.
16. Yoma 10a.
17. Megilah 1:9.
18. Ezekiel 38:8.
19. Malbim Ezekiel 38:23 and Zechariah 12:2; Rashi Zechariah 13:9.

20. Siforno Psalms 83; Malbim Ezekiel 38:2; Radak Zechariah 12.
21. Malbim Ezekiel 38:2.
22. Lev Eliyahu Yisro, p. 172.
23. *Bar Kokhba*, p. 257.
24. Isaiah 11:4.
25. Ibid.
26. Ezekiel 38:9.
27. *Igres Moshe Orech Chaim* IV, no. 81.
28. Ezekiel 38:23.
29. Ibid. 39:12.
30. Rashi and Targum Ezekiel 39:11.
31. Melochim 12:2.
32. Likutim no. 88.
33. Sucah 52b.
34. Tzav 9:6.

CHAPTER 32

1. Malachi 3:24.
2. Tosfos Eruvin 43b, implying that Elijah will appear before the Messiah comes.
3. Ramban Milchemes Hashem 24, also implying that Elijah will precede the Messiah.
4. Rashi Malachi 3:24.
5. Mishna Idyos 8:7; Maimonides, Melochim 12:2.
6. Mechiltah Shilach 16:33.
7. Metzudos David Malachi 3:24.
8. Ridvaz Sanhedrin 4:11.
9. Rebbe Shimon, Mishna Idyos 8:7.
10. Milchemes Hashem 24.
11. Melochim 14:2.
12. Likutim no. 88.

CHAPTER 33

1. Berochos 34b.
2. Isaiah 2:2,4.
3. Maimonides, Teshuva 9:2.
4. Maimonides, Melochim 12:5.
5. Maharal Netzach Yisroel 3.
6. Isaiah 11:9.
7. Maimonides Teshuva 11:4.
8. Isaiah 11:6.
9. Melochim 12:1.
10. Leviticus 26:6.
11. Sanhedrin 99a.
12. Ibid.
13. Ibid.
14. Another version; ibid.
15. Ibid.
16. Ibid. 97a.
17. Ibid. 99a.
18. Ibid.
19. Ibid.
20. A version quoted by Rashi; ibid.

CHAPTER 34

1. Daniel 12:2.
2. Daniel 12:12.
3. Taanis 30b and Rosh HaShana 16b.
4. Radvaz III:1069 and Migdol David 83a.
5. *Igeres Techias HaMaysim.*
6. Shar HaGomul.
7. Rahn Sanhedrin 89a.
8. Nidah 61b.

CHAPTER 35

1. Isaiah 2:2,3.
2. Maaser Sheni 5:2.
3. Megilah 17b.
4. Melochim 11:1,4.

CHAPTER 36

1. Sanhedrin 89b.
2. Sucah 52a.
3. Chasam Sofer 6:98.
4. Sanhedrin 110b.
5. Ibid 89b.

CHAPTER 37

1. Melochim 11:4.

CHAPTER 38

1. Rabbi Ovadiah Bartenurah, in his commentary to Ruth, says that in each generation there is an individual, a descendant of the Davidic dynasty, who could qualify to be the Messiah. The Talmud (Sanhedrin 98a) records that Rebbe Yehoshua ben Levi found the Messiah at the gateway of the city. Though the Vilna Goan says that it refers to Rome, Rashi, quoting his teachers, says that it refers to the entrance of the Garden of Eden. Ramban, in his Book of Disputation, concurs with Rashi's teachers. The symbolic significance of the Garden of Eden is that anyone found within its boundaries cannot die. The implication is that the Messiah is a particular individual

who resides in Eden. He cannot die. When the time is right, he will leave to reveal himself to the world. The Jerusalem Talmud (Berochos 1:4) says the Messiah was born the day the Temple was destroyed. This too implies that the Messiah is a particular individual.

2. "As it was in former times" probably means that the Davidic monarchy will be established over all of Israel as it was in the time of David and Solomon, before the land was divided into two kingdoms.

3. From the sequence of Maimonides' wording, it seems that the Temple will be rebuilt before the ingathering of the Diaspora takes place. Maharsha (Megilah 17b) states that just as in the time of the First Temple, the Jews gathered into the land of Israel after conquering it and then built the Temple, so too in the future, the ingathering will occur first then the Messiah will rebuild the Temple.

4. "Justice will be revived . . . as in former times" probably refers to the reinstitution of rabbinical ordination.

5. Maimonides is implying that the observance of the Sabbatical year in our times is only by rabbinical edict.

6. Ramban, in his Book of Disputation, writes: "[The Messiah] will come before the Pope and all the kings of the nations in the name of God, [declaring] 'Send forth My nation so they may serve Me.' He will perform great wonders and will have no fear of them at all."

Ramban is saying that the Messiah will perform miracles as a sign of his true indentity.

In the Commentary to Song of Songs, attributed to Rabaynu Saadyia Goan, it states that the Jews will not have faith in the Messiah the son of David until he brings back to life the Messiah the son of Joseph. Rav Hai Goan in his Responsae records a similar midrashic legend.

In Saadyia Goan's Beliefs and Opinions (ch. 3) he writes that the Messiah will not be confirmed until after he does wonders.

Rabbi Yosef Albo (Ikrim, ch. 18) writes that the Messiah will be tested by being required to perform miracles or predict the future.

It could be explained that all the above opinions are based on a Midrash that states Messiah the son of David will resurrect the Messiah the son of Joseph. Maimonides does not make any reference to the Messiah the son of Joseph and therefore does not agree with that Midrash.

However, Maimonides himself implies that the Messiah will be required to perform miracles. In his Letter to Yemen he writes: An unknown man will arise before his [messianic] identity [is revealed] and the signs and wonders that will be seen through his hand, they will prove his true claim.

Perhaps, Maimonides does not refer to supernatural miracles, but rather to the military successes the Messiah will bring about. This seems to be the very reason Rebbe Akiva endorsed Bar Kokhba.

7. These last two sentences do not seem to fit with the previous matter. Undoubtedly, there is a lacuna due to censorship. The original text must have alluded to the fact that the Christian and Moslem messianic figures abolished the commandments of the "Old Testament" and ordained revised requirements in a new testament. Maimonides is stating that this view of Messiah's authority is contrary to Judaic philosophy and contradicts the Torah itself.

8. Though Maimonides makes no mention here of Messiah's prophetic abilities, in his "Laws of Repentance" (9:2) he writes: "[The Messiah] will possess wisdom greater than Solomon and possess prophetic abilities approaching those of our teacher Moses."

It is curious that Maimonides makes no mention here of the Messiah's ability to prophesy. It is also peculiar that there is no indication that Bar Kokhba had this ability. In the chapter entitled "Was Rebbe Akiva Wrong?" I mentioned that there are two stages to the recognition of the Messianic figure. The first is called the "assumed Messiah." The second stage is called the "certain Messiah." In this line, Maimonides is describing the "assumed Messiah." Prophetic abilities are not required to be recognized as an "assumed Messiah." Rebbe Akiva likewise did not require any demonstration of prophetic ability from Bar Kokhba to be endorsed as an "assumed Messiah."

9. Though it is known that the Temple must be built on the Temple Mount (Mount Moriah), the exact location of the Altar and the other Temple structures is not known. The Messiah will ascertain that the structures are built in their correct place.

10. Rabbi Menachem Kasher (*Tekifah HaGedolah*, p. 343) explains Maimonides' comment to refer to the many persecutions, forced conversions, and slaughters the Jews had to endure from the followers of the Christian and Moslem messiahs.

It may be of significance to note that although Judaism obviously does not recognize the claims of the Christian messiah and of the Moslem prophet, one noteworthy aspect came about through them. Prior to the advent of these two religions, all the nations except Israel served idolatry and paganism. As a result of Christianity and Islam, large segments of the non-Jewish world rejected idolatry and paganism. Previously, only Judaism accepted the notion of a future Messiah who would unite the world and bring human history to its climax. Christianity and Islam spread the messianic concept abroad.

11. Raavad (ibid.) assumes the verse to be taken literally.

12. It is unclear what Maimonides considers permissible food for non-Jews. Perhaps he refers to the fact non-Jews are prohibited from eating the flesh of a live animal. That would explain the following verse, for it is the way of the lion to eat from its prey while it is still alive.

13. See footnote 6.

Bibliography

Avi-Yonah, Michael. *The Jews of Palestine*. New York: Schocken Books, 1976.

Avigad, Nachum. "The Burial Vault of a Nrzirite Family on Mount Scopus." *Israel Exploration Journal* 21 (1971): 166–167.

Chiyon, Yehudah. *Otzer Acharis HaYomim*. Bnai Brak, Israel, 1993.

Cornfeld, G. *Josephus, The Jewish War*. Grand Rapids, MI: Zondervan, 1982.

Eisenstein, J. D. *Otzer Yisroel*. New York: Pardes, 1952.

Flavius, Josephus. *Antiquities of the Jews*. Trans. W. Whiston. Philadelphia: John C. Winston Co., 1957.

Graetz, H. *History of the Jews*. Philadelphia: Jewish Publication Society, 1956.

Haas, N. "Anthropological Observations on the Skeletal Remains from Givat ha-Mivtar." *Israel Exploration Journal* 20 (1970).

Kloner, A. "Name of Ancient Israel's Last President Discovered on Lead Weight." *Biblical Archaeological Review* 4 (1988): 12–17.

Mare, W. H. *The Archaeology of the Jerusalem Area*. Grand Rapids, MI: Baker Book House, 1987.

Mazar, B. *The Mountain of the Lord*. Garden City, NY: Doubleday, 1975.

McCarter, P. K. "Let's Be Serious about the Bat Creek Stone." *Biblical Archaeological Review* 19 (1993): 54–55.

McCulloch, J. H. "Did Judean Refugees Escape to Tennessee?" *Biblical Archaeological Review* 19 (1993): 46–53.

Naveh, J. "An Aramaic Tomb Inscription Written in Paleo-Hebrew Script." *Israel Exploration Journal* 23 (1973): 82–91.

Netzer, E. "Searching for Herod's Tomb." *Biblical Archaeological Review* 9:3 (1983): 30–51.

———. *Herodium: An Archaeological Guide*. Jerusalem: Cana, 1987.

———. "Jewish Rebels Dig Strategic Tunnel System." *Biblical Archaeological Review* 15:4 (1988): 18–33.

Patrich, J. "Hideouts in the Judean Wilderness." *Biblical Archaeological Review* 15:5 (1989): 32–42.

Reznick, L. *The Holy Temple Revisited*. Northvale, NJ: Jason Aronson Inc., 1990.

———. "Hidden Blue." *Jewish Action* 51:1 (1991): 53–57.

———. *A Time to Weep*. Lakewood, NJ: CIS Publishers, 1993.

Rosenthal, E. S. "The Givat ha-Mivtar Inscription." *Israel Exploration Journal* 23 (1973): 72–81.

Shanks, H. *Judaism in Stone*. New York: Harper and Row, 1979.

———. "Carbon-14 Tests Substantiate Scroll Dates." *Biblical Archaeological Review* 17:6 (1991): 72.

Sharon, A. *Planning Jerusalem*. New York: McGraw Hill, 1973.

Tabor, J. "The Pierced or Piercing Messiah." *Biblical Archaeological Review* 18:6 (1992): 58–59.

Tzaferis, V. "Tombs at and near Givat ha-Mivtar." *Israel Exploration Journal* 20 (1970): 18–32.

Wise, M., and Tabor, J. "The Messiah at Qumran." *Biblical Archaeological Review* 18:6 (1992): 60–65.

Yadin, Y. *Jerusalem Revealed*. Jerusalem: Israel Exploration Society, 1975.

———. *Bar Kokhba*. London: Weidenfeld and Nicolson, 1978.

———. *The Temple Scroll*. New York: Random House, 1985.

Index

About the Author

Rabbi Leibel Reznick is a lecturer in the Beth Medresh division of Shaarei Torah of Rockland County, New York. He is the author of *The Holy Temple Revisited, Woe Jerusalem!*, and *A Time to Weep*. He has also written more than 100 magazine and newspaper articles on Jewish history, archaeology, theology, and social commentary. Rabbi Reznick received his ordination from the Beth Medresh Elyon Institute of Spring Valley, New York, and is known for his unique interpretation of secular ancient history and modern archaeological finds in the light of traditional rabbinic sources. The rabbi lives in Rockland County, New York, with his wife, Shoshana. They have five children living in New York and Israel.